PEOPLE OF THE TONTO RIM

The work at Shoofly Village benefited in many ways from the close interaction of professional archaeologists with local amateurs and the general public. This book is dedicated to the continuation of this valuable partnership in pursuit of a better understanding of the past.

Charles L. Redman

PEOPLE OF THE
TONTO RIM

ARCHAEOLOGICAL DISCOVERY

IN PREHISTORIC ARIZONA

SMITHSONIAN INSTITUTION PRESS

Washington and London

© 1993 Smithsonian Institution
All rights reserved
Printed in the United States
Editor: Nancy L. Benco
Designer: Alan Carter

Library of Congress Cataloging-in-Publication Data

Redman, Charles L.
   People of the Tonto Rim : archaeological discovery in
prehistoric Arizona / Charles L. Redman.
      p.   cm.
   Includes bibliographical references and index.
   ISBN 1-56098-193-8 (casebound : alk. paper). — ISBN
1-56098-192-X (pbk. : alk. paper)
      1. Shoofly Village Site (Ariz.)   2. Indians of North
America—Arizona—Payson Region—Antiquities.
   3. Excavations (Archaeology)—Arizona—Payson Region.
   4. Payson Region (Ariz.)—Antiquities.
      I. Title.
   E78.A7R44   1993
   979.1'55—dc20   92-25213
                                                   CIP

∞ The paper in this book meets the requirements of the
American National Standard for Permanence of Paper for
Printed Materials Z39.48-1984

Cover illustration shows a reconstruction of Shoofly Village
Ruins, by artist Jon Joha

Contents

Acknowledgments

The successful conduct of an archaeological project relies on the efforts of many people and, hence, recognition for this book should go far beyond its author. Many of these people will be cited in the text when I draw directly on their writings, but others will not be included in this way, although they have played an essential role in the Payson project and in the formulation of my ideas.

We would never have approached Shoofly Village or been able to carry out our work in such a smooth fashion without the constant support of the personnel of the Tonto National Forest, especially forest archaeologists Martin McAllister and J. Scott Wood. Primary financial support for the investigation of the many small sites in the Payson region was provided by Federal Land Exchange, Inc., under the direction of Norval Tyler. My archaeological colleagues at Arizona State University were instrumental in getting the field school at Shoofly Village off the ground and in contributing their insights at various points.

In attempting to convey the full richness of the archaeological past, yet to avoid endless pages of descriptive information, I have chosen to include many maps, architectural plans, and interpretive summaries but have minimized the presentation of actual raw counts of artifacts and exact measurements of features. For the serious archaeology student or teacher, however, this detailed information would be useful for conducting further studies or even for testing ideas I have presented here. Consequently, a detailed data bank of provenience information and artifact counts for Shoofly Village and the other excavated sites mentioned in this volume is available at a modest cost by writing directly to the author at Arizona State University. The information will be provided on floppy disks in a generalized format suitable for input into most database programs and will include descriptive information for the user. Another issue of facilitating communication with the reader and professional alike was to standardize the use of English and metric systems of measurement. My own solution has been to maintain the English system for Chapters 1 to 3 where we are dealing with regional maps based on U.S. Geological Survey maps and employ the metric system for Chapters 4 to 10 following standard practice for archaeological excavation information.

Without any question the key element in the success of the Payson project has been the dedication of its staff of graduate students and visiting scholars. These people provided careful direction for the student excavators, carried out important research projects on the material recovered, and did the many practical jobs that kept this large and complex project running. Throughout this book you will find information and ideas that originated or were developed in conjunction with one or another staff member. I was fortunate that Patricia Gilman and Paul Minnis took time out from their other academic duties to direct the field school during the summer of 1986. I was also fortunate to have assembled a talented group of graduate students who were able to take on the day-to-day responsibilities of the fieldwork and many of the intellectual responsibilities of the analysis. Owen Lindauer, R. Jane Bradley, and John Hohmann each distinguished themselves in directing much of the research that occurred, and they will be cited frequently throughout this volume.

Among the many tasks associated with the project were field photography, recording architectural plans, drafting illustrations, and assembling this manuscript. Some of the many individuals who contributed in these ways were David Eshbaugh, John Hohmann, Jon Joha, Owen Lindauer, Greg Phillips, Marsha Schweitzer, Sharon Vaughn, Elizabeth Welsh, and Linda Williams. Beyond these, there were more than a dozen additional staff members and over 100 field school students and contract workers who devoted themselves for one or more seasons to unlocking the secrets of the prehistoric sites of the

Payson region. We were also fortunate to have the active participation of amateur archaeologists from the Payson area and around the state. Their continuing interest in the archaeology of the region led to the formation of a Shoofly Chapter of the Arizona Archaeological Society centered in Payson, and its members are now carrying on their own fieldwork.

Hence, it is because of my association with these many hard working and enthusiastic people that I have been able to assemble the information and ideas that form the basis of this book. Just as this book tells the story of groups of industrious people who lived in central Arizona more than 800 years ago, their story could not have been written without the efforts of another equally industrious group of people who came together in an effort to better know the past.

1 □□□□ The Story of an Archaeological Project

This book tells the story of what has been learned about the people who lived from about A.D. 1000 to A.D. 1300 in the region around the modern towns of Payson and Star Valley in central Arizona. It is a story that was virtually unknown until recent archaeological research revealed details about the prehistoric peoples and communities in the region. It is also the story of the archaeological adventure during which scholars, students, and volunteers worked under the auspices of the Tonto National Forest and Arizona State University (ASU) to expand our understanding of the prehistory of central Arizona.

In the fall of 1983, Tonto National Forest archaeologists Martin McAllister and J. Scott Wood took me on a visit to a site known as the Shoofly Village Ruins, which is located 4 mi northeast of Payson, and suggested that it was a very promising site for excavation (Fig. 1.1). I was seeking a large prehistoric settlement that exhibited characteristics of a relatively complex society and was suitable for a major archaeological research project and field school for ASU. Although I had examined sites in other parts of Arizona, I concluded that Shoofly Village offered the best combination of research interpretive potential and practical conditions.[1] Situated at an intermediate elevation near one of the main

1

2 CHARLES L. REDMAN

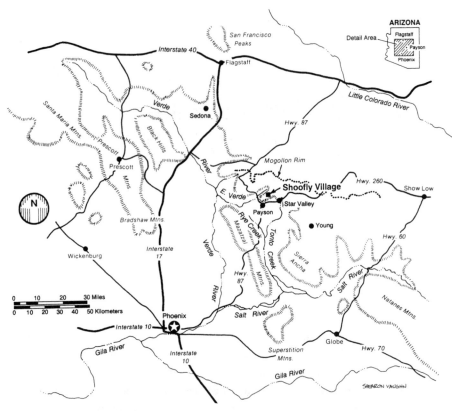

1.1 Map of central Arizona with location of Shoofly Village Ruins.

prehistoric north-south land routes between the desert territory of the
Hohokam people and the Colorado Plateau country of the Anasazi,
Shoofly Village held the potential for revealing characteristics of one or
both of these important groups in a new locale or of showing that the
village represented some sort of combination of the two. In addition,
Shoofly Village's high mesa-top location was between the headwaters of
two major drainages: the Verde River, which led into the heart of the
land inhabited by the southern Sinagua people, and Tonto Creek,
which watered the land of the people called Salado. This pivotal geographic and demographic position was made even more attractive, for
my purposes, by the logistical advantages that the location of Shoofly
Village offered. Relatively close to a paved road and not far from

present-day Payson, it promised to allow the maximum energy of the project to be devoted to research aims.

Shoofly Village covered about five acres and had surface indications of abundant architecture and artifacts (Fig. 1.2). The surface remains were especially intriguing. They indicated that the prehistoric settlement consisted of rooms of various shapes, arranged into groups that were each organized into a different pattern, and yet the entire village was surrounded by an uninterrupted compound wall. The presence of different architectural styles within a single site is very unusual for the Southwest, or for any region. More than any other single factor, it was Shoofly Village's architectural distinctiveness and diversity that made the site so compelling, and it is that same diversity, now better understood, that stimulated me to write this book.

Early Archaeological Research in the Payson-Star Valley Area

Until recently, the Payson-Star Valley area has not been the focus of substantial archaeological activity. This is probably due in part to the region's undecorated prehistoric ceramics, which failed to capture the attention of professional researchers or amateur archaeologists. In addition, the region has generally been portrayed as being on the periphery of an area inhabited by one of the better known culture groups, such as the Sinagua or Salado, and, consequently, little direct discussion of the Payson-Star Valley area's own characteristics have been published.

The first published archaeological research on the Payson-Star Valley area was an archaeological survey conducted in 1954 by Alan and Frances Olson for Chicago's Field Museum (Olson and Olson 1954). Their study area extended roughly from the towns of Payson and Pine to Kohl's Ranch. The Olsons recorded 55 sites, including pueblos, single-room sites, pithouses, and artifact scatters. Although their work was most concerned with larger sites, it was clear from their survey that this region contained many smaller sites as well. In 1955, Fred Peck conducted an archaeological survey along the length of the East Verde River (Peck 1956), and in 1967, Roger Kelly of the Museum of Northern Arizona completed another survey near Payson in the vicinity of a proposed seismological observatory (Kelly 1969).

1.2   View from Shoofly Village towards Tonto Rim to the north.

Improvements made to State Route 87, the Beeline Highway, prompted additional archaeological work in the region. During a survey in 1967, Laurens Hammack found several sites in an area extending from Rye to Ox Bow Hill south of Payson (Hammack 1969). Ten years later an Arizona State Museum project excavated four sites located between Payson and the sites previously found by Hammack (Huckell 1978). At one of these sites the excavators believe that they uncovered evidence of a Clovis period occupation that could be dated to as early as 9000 B.C. (Huckell 1978). In 1989, William Doelle led a large project to excavate several additional sites just south of Rye (Elson 1989). Doelle's work completed a geographic transect that follows State Route 87 from the higher elevation zone of Payson to the lower elevation of the Tonto Basin.

Interest in the Payson region among ASU's archaeologists began in the early 1970s when a series of ASU field schools under Ed Dittert's overall direction were held in the area (Dittert 1975, 1976; Jeter 1978; Lightfoot, Abbott, and Prager-Bergman 1977). In cooperation with the Tonto National Forest, the ASU team conducted several archaeological surveys and excavated a number of small sites. Among the sites that the survey team visited in 1975 was Shoofly Village Ruins; the team mapped the site and collected a sample of surface artifacts for dating purposes and to evaluate trade connections (Most 1975). In 1978, the ASU field school left the area. Archaeological work in the region slowed until 1984 when scholars and students, under the auspices of ASU, returned to spend the next four summers working at Shoofly Village Ruins and at more than 70 other sites in the region (Hohmann and Redman 1988; Lindauer, Bradley, and Redman 1991; Redman, Bradley, and Lindauer 1987; Redman and Hohmann 1986). These sites included large masonry settlements, such as Shoofly Village, small masonry hamlets, pithouse clusters, and artifact scatters. Most of the regional prehistory presented here is based on these excavations.

The Adventure of Archaeological Fieldwork

Although this book is largely the story of the people who lived at Shoofly Village some 800 years ago, it is also the story of the dig itself.[2] Archaeology is a fascinating discipline, partly because it is so challenging, defying simple solutions. Increasingly, modern science is being used to help analyze archaeological remains. Yet even with the best help technology can offer, interpretations of the past require judgment, the ability to integrate diverse scientific findings, and imaginative insights into how people might have lived. It is the combination of modern scientific technology with a humanistic perspective that makes archaeology fascinating.

Knowledge of the prehistoric past emanates largely from what is under the ground. Most archaeological information is gathered through the survey and excavation of ancient sites. Although we are constantly inventing new methods for predicting what will be found below the ground's surface, we can never know with certainty what awaits us, and, thus, there is a sense of discovery that accompanies every archaeological field project. It is all of these aspects—science, the humanities, and the promise of discovery—taken together that make an archaeological field project one of the great adventures of a lifetime.

The Shoofly Village project was able to offer these opportunities to a diverse group of participants. Undergraduate and graduate students were recruited from across the country and abroad to attend the ASU field school and spend part of their summer digging, analyzing, and interpreting the past (Fig. 1.3). For some, it would be their only exposure to field archaeology in a broad liberal arts training program. For others, it was a necessary component of professional training in archaeology: a field project provides the student with the hands-on experience that no amount of book learning can replace. For more advanced graduate students, it was an opportunity to apply what they had learned in order to improve our understanding of the people of central Arizona.

As is increasingly the case in North American archaeology, a component of the project was to conduct fieldwork on a contract basis. Land in the vicinity of Shoofly Village administered by the Tonto National Forest was to be transferred to a private developer, Federal Land Exchange, Inc., in trade for other land deemed more necessary by U.S. Forest Service officials. Before this exchange could be completed, federal laws required that the archaeological resources on the national forest land be assessed. This land exchange contract thereby provided us with the opportunity to examine many other sites in the Payson-Star Valley area, and the payment that ASU received for this contract work provided supplemental financial support for some of the students and staff taking part in the field school.

An archaeological field school resembles a small city, although it is often located far from modern conveniences. Life revolves around the excavation and laboratory processing of archaeological finds. People come to know one another well and learn to work together, sometimes under difficult conditions. More importantly, they establish a relationship with the environment and, perhaps, even with the archaeological site far beyond anything possible in a classroom or office setting. This direct contact contributes to the field archaeologist's capacity to understand the site's past.

Scholars and university students were not the only ones involved in the field experience at Shoofly Village. Archaeology has a long and close relationship with the public, and public involvement has been especially important on the Shoofly Village project. The overarching goal of the earliest anthropologists—and archaeologists—was to discover and describe the full diversity of human existence, past and present. The excitement inherent in this quest was shared by scientists and

1.3   Graduate student
cleaning prehistoric wall
during excavations at
Shoofly Village.

the public alike. The public set North American archaeology on its course a century ago, and today the public is still playing an active role in charting its future (Redman 1989; Rogge 1989). At Shoofly Village, we hosted special field schools for the public under the auspices of the Arizona Archaeological Society, a statewide amateur archaeology group. We also pioneered the concept of an archaeological "open house," in which the public was invited to the site to witness our ongoing archaeological project, talk with excavators at work, and take part in the dig while under close supervision. This has been a tremendously successful program, growing each year in attendance and acclaim.

Open houses are beneficial for the archaeologists as well. In order to answer the probing questions of nonspecialist visitors, archaeologists are forced to crystallize their ideas about the past and how they are pursuing it. Hence, Shoofly Village served not only as a training ground for future archaeologists at a location where the public was able to learn about archaeology but also as a testing ground for renewed interaction between the public and the professionals. It is in the hope of furthering that stimulating interaction that this volume was written.

Notes

1. The designation for Shoofly Village Ruins (also known as Houston Mesa Ruins) in the Arizona State Museum site files is AZ 0:11:6 (ASU). The Tonto National Forest maintains a separate inventory of site designations, where Shoofly Village is AR-03-12-04-20. In this volume we have used the U.S. Forest Service numbering system and have referred to unnamed sites by the last three digits of the designation (e.g., Site 620 is AR-03-12-04-620).

2. For more insights into the excitement and difficulties of fieldwork, the reader is referred to a variety of fascinating books on the subject. Some works focus on the actual conduct of the dig, such as the reflections of Sir Leonard Woolley concerning his work at Ur (1954) and those of a group of distinguished fieldworkers assembled by Gordon Willey (1974). Probably of even greater interest are the books written by the talented wives of excavators who attempted to blend information on the excavations with aspects of life in a field camp and associated adventures. Works by Linda Braidwood (1953), Ann Morris (1933), and many others offer fascinating insights, but, for the neophyte archaeologist, my very favorite account is by Agatha Christie who relates her own exposure to archaeology in a volume entitled, *Come Tell Me How You Live* (1946).

2 □ □ □ □   *An Archaeological Perspective on Arizona's Past*

The past serves as an anchor for the present. It shows us how we came to be who we are and, perhaps, hints at where we are going as a society. It is the past that gives us our identity, our perspective, and our vision of the future. The past tells of the diversity of our predecessors, their achievements, and their failings. It is a record of conflict and cooperation and of countless generations of human use and misuse of the environment. The past reveals the lifeways of earlier people, from incidents of innovation and discovery to the solutions for everyday problems faced by ordinary people. In the American Southwest the past is the story of the entry of the first peoples into this land, the learning of agriculture, the spread of diseases, and the development and refinement of many adaptations in order to live successfully in a sometimes hostile environment. The greater part of the evidence of the past, however, reveals the stability of routine activities, normal people living their lives to the fullest and experiencing the same personal needs, feelings, hopes, and fears that we have today.

We come to know the past in many ways. Written documents detail many of the events of recent years. Oral histories are retold from one generation to the next to recount ancestry and to teach and preserve a society's accumulated knowledge. Oral histories are especially valuable for our study of the past in places where there has been a long continuity of settlement. Ethnographic accounts, which describe the lifeways of contemporary peoples, are another source of insights into the past, particularly when the modern group has an affiliation with the people whose past is being reconstructed.

There are, however, large parts of the Southwest that were abandoned by prehistoric occupants centuries ago and were reoccupied by new groups at a later time. This is the case for much of central Arizona, including the region around the modern towns of Payson and Star Valley. There are no contemporary Indian groups who identify themselves as direct descendants of the people who lived in Shoofly Village or in other Payson-area settlements of that time period. For an understanding of the prehistoric groups who lived around Payson, there are no historical texts, oral traditions, or ethnographic continuities. To uncover their past, we must rely completely on the actual material remains that they left behind, accessible to us only through archaeology. Because of this relatively limited means, some details may be undiscoverable. Archaeology, however, is a complex science that examines all aspects of the fragmentary remains of past peoples and is often able to reconstruct an unknown era with surprising clarity. Archaeologists combine forces with geologists, botanists, zoologists, chemists, and anthropologists to bring to bear the full potential of modern science for unlocking the secrets of the past.

A New Perspective on Southwestern Archaeology and Cultural Traditions

Although archaeological research in the American Southwest began more than 100 years ago, the Southwest is still one of the most actively investigated regions of the world. Every year dozens of field projects and scores of exciting discoveries are reported in popular and scholarly publications. In the four states that comprise the American Southwest—Arizona, New Mexico, Utah, and Colorado—there are 24 archaeological national parks and monuments. The Southwest is also home to the largest concentration of contemporary American Indians, many of whom trace their ancestry directly to the prehistoric peoples of the region. Together, these factors have led to a widespread appreciation of the great achievements of the early peoples of the Southwest (Fig. 2.1).

The best known and most widely written about Southwestern cultural tradition belongs to the Anasazi. The Anasazi were the great builders of Mesa Verde, Chaco Canyon, and many other settlements so remarkable that they are now protected as national monuments; they are also responsible for thousands of lesser well-known sites. The Hopis and Zunis are among the contemporary Indian groups that consider the Anasazi to be their ancestors. For many years, Anasazi was the cultural heritage automatically associated with the prehistoric Southwest.

During the past 20 years, however, there has been a great expansion of archaeological work in the Southwest, particularly in areas where there has been rapid urban growth. Primary among these areas have been the desert valleys of the Salt and Gila rivers and their major tributaries in southern Arizona. This has resulted in an enormous increase in our knowledge about the Hohokam, the prehistoric irrigation agriculturalists of the Sonoran desert (Gumerman 1991; Haury 1976). Although they built their architecture using mud that has not endured as well as the stone masonry of the Anasazi, we have recently come to recognize that the achievements of the Hohokam were no less grand, and the society they created was, in many ways, one of the most sophisticated in all of North America (Crown and Judge 1991).

Given their prehistoric technology, the ability of the Anasazi and Hohokam to settle in regions of the Southwest that most of us would consider inhospitable is as remarkable as their striking artifacts and spectacular buildings. The Anasazi discovered how to get the most out of the scattered water sources of the otherwise dry Colorado Plateau and to build substantial homes that sheltered them through the cold winters of their territory. The Hohokam invented irrigation techniques that enabled them to farm in otherwise arid environments and built housing that helped them survive the extreme summer heat of Arizona's southern deserts.

But what of the less difficult environments of the Southwest, and of Arizona in particular? There is a vast area between the cold heights of the White Mountains and Colorado Plateau and the hot dry deserts of

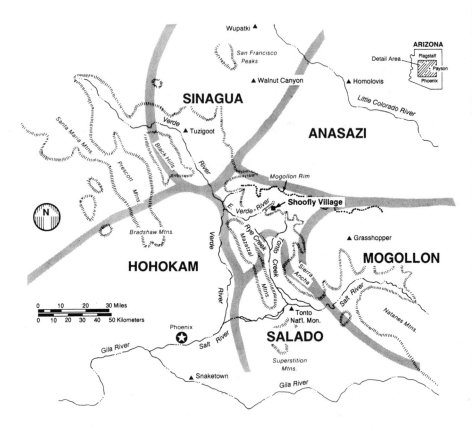

2.1   Core areas of prehistoric cultural traditions in central Arizona. Note
Shoofly Village is near to, but not located within, the boundaries of well-
defined traditions.

the south and west. For the prehistoric Indians of Arizona who had to
contend directly with the climate, life would have been far easier at
these intermediate elevations. This temperate area stretches from the
present-day towns of Prescott and Sedona on the west, past Payson and
Young in the center, to Safford and Willcox in the southeast. This is the
region that early Anglo settlers found most hospitable for farming and
grazing livestock, and where many of today's desert residents spend
summer weekends; others live there year-round because of the pleasant
summers and moderate winters. As a region, it receives the highest
rainfall in Arizona, supporting abundant wild flora and fauna.

For prehistoric people with modest technological advantages, the central region permitted a comparatively easy life. Rainfall-watered agriculture and the hunting and gathering of wild resources provided food for scattered villages, and the absence of climatic extremes allowed relatively simple house construction.

Although archaeologists have found numerous prehistoric sites throughout the central region, relatively little has been written about these discoveries (Spoerl and Gumerman 1983). Unable to formulate one clear-cut definition of the people who lived in these settlements, archaeologists have often assigned the sites they discovered in central Arizona to such groups as the southern Sinagua, the Salado, or the Western Mogollon—cultural traditions whose core areas were located outside the central area (see Figure 2.1). Each of these designations is associated with characteristic artifacts or other cultural traits. Although many settlements in central Arizona appear to fit into these categories, there are an equal number that do not fit neatly into any of these divisions.

A cultural tradition is usually identified by archaeologists when various elements of the cultural repertoire, such as pottery making, house construction, and burial customs, are uniformly followed for a substantial period of time by many neighboring groups. A cultural tradition is often associated with the presence of strong social or political control over the way people carried out their work, control which fostered consistency in the way things were done. Strong social control can allow people to successfully inhabit an otherwise hostile environment by regulating their activities and causing a more complex social and economic order to develop.

One of the important lessons we are learning from investigating the emergence of increasingly complex social and economic orders is that these types of development did not always improve the likelihood of a group's survival. History has shown us that in complex societies decisions are often made that maximize short-term economic benefits but endanger long-term survival (Redman 1992). For instance, during several periods in Mesopotamian history, highly centralized states are known to have compromised their future agricultural productivity by overspecializing in limited crops and using techniques that had long-term negative impacts. Although they sometimes rose to tremendous wealth and political power, these complex states typically succumbed to disintegrative forces after a relatively short period of florescence. By contrast, as Robert Adams (1978) has pointed out, other smaller scale social groups proved to be more enduring by retaining a diversity in the food sources they relied upon. These seemingly less prosperous groups never matched the productivity of the highly centralized states, but their cultural resilience provided a more stable lifeway that lasted for centuries. In fact, it can be argued that the more stable lifeway in smaller communities maintained a society's values and identity during periods of state collapse. Thus, these less complex but more enduring societies ensured the re-emergence of successive Mesopotamian and Near Eastern states.

A parallel situation may have existed in the American Southwest. Clearly, the Anasazi and the Hohokam were societies with complex forms of social control and major economic successes. Their innovations in organizing society allowed them to support dense aggregations of people, broad political alliances, far-flung trade networks, and some form of social stratification (Crown and Judge 1991).

These achievements, however, were relatively short-lived. Although there is a long buildup preceding their florescence, the Anasazi's real heyday in any specific region, such as Chaco Canyon, may have lasted as little as one century. For the Hohokam, the period of florescence seems to have lasted longer, although current opinion (Crown and Judge 1991) contends that what appears to be a long period of social and economic achievement really consisted of separate episodes between which small-scale societies predominated—a situation strikingly similar to that in early Mesopotamia. In Arizona, the persistent, steadily successful small-scale societies seem to have included the peoples in central Arizona whose cultural identification has been so elusive.

Despite these tantalizing similarities, there is a crucial difference between cultural florescence in Mesopotamia and in the Southwest. The social and political institutions that developed in Mesopotamia during the city-state period continued to grow in power and influence even after individual states declined, and these social and political systems formed the structure out of which increasingly complex state-level societies grew. This was not the case, however, in the American Southwest where the new social orders developed by the Anasazi and Hohokam failed to persist for long periods of time and ultimately dissolved. Throughout the Southwest, most groups reverted to looser social controls, smaller community size, and less intensive subsistence strategies after their period of economic and political florescence. In many regions, such as the Payson-Star Valley area, this downsizing ultimately led to an outright abandonment of the land and a consequent loss of social identity long before the disruptive entrance of Europeans.

Although the nature of social organization among the Anasazi and Hohokam is not the main subject of this volume, I will outline a few patterns in these cultural traditions that contrast sharply with those in the prehistoric settlements around Payson-Star Valley and, I expect, throughout much of central Arizona. One hallmark of a relatively complex society in many regions of the world, including the Anasazi and Hohokam areas, is the presence of highly standardized pottery and uniformly constructed settlements. These are obvious results of shared ideas and the existence of a core group of individuals with sufficient influence to impose these ideas on the productive segments of society. Moreover, the standardization in crafts is sometimes reflective of their production by specialists, some of whom may have been directly controlled by members of the core group.

Among the Anasazi, architectural uniformity included the repetition of structural units in their settlements, or pueblos. The typical Anasazi habitation site, as we know it from archaeology, ranged from small clusters of several similar-looking dwellings, or "unit pueblos," to very large sites in which a myriad of small rooms were neatly aligned. In both cases, the repetition of similar architectural components was the essence of the settlement, and perhaps helped to implement the relatively rigid social control I have hypothesized.

Hohokam communities consisted of numerous, similar-looking clusters of houses that formed sprawling settlements along major irrigation canals. The autonomy of individual house clusters, which were sometimes enclosed by compound walls in a Hohokam settlement, may have been greater than those within an Anasazi settlement. But I would argue that the overall architectural uniformity of these communities may reflect an attempt by a newly formed elite to control a large population and maximize the centralization of production. However, I

believe that this uniformity and central control also contributed to the
fragility of the Hohokam and Anasazi cultures in the face of changing
circumstances and led to their eventual demise.

The achievements of the Hohokam and Anasazi societies have
attracted the enthusiasm of countless archaeologists. Their distinctive
cultural trappings make cultural definitions relatively easy and clear-
cut. The nonspecialist audience also finds it rewarding to learn about
societies with recognizable features that occur over and over again,
especially if they are appealing. It is the combination of rich cultural
material with recurring, easily identifiable cultural markers that have
made these "great cultural traditions" of the American Southwest the
focus of most studies, almost to the exclusion of other societies in the
area.

But do they represent the essential, enduring Southwestern prehistoric lifeway? It is my opinion that they do not, or at least in these cases
the essential lifeway is masked by other, more transitory patterns. It
seems to me that the peak decades of these "great cultural tradition"
societies represent only temporary, albeit magnificent, responses to specific environmental constraints and economic opportunities. They were
unquestionably "Southwestern" responses and are well worth studying. But I would argue that they *emerged out of* what was truly characteristic Southwestern society and, when their experimental systems col-
lapsed, groups of people returned to their more enduring "natural"
Southwestern way of life. The A.D. 1100–1300 occupation period in the
Payson-Star Valley area appears to be a successful, yet uncomplicated,
example of this "natural" Southwestern lifeway.

The Enduring Cultural Tradition of the Southwest

My belief is that many widespread groups share a set of cultural traits
that characterize and define the enduring, essential prehistoric Southwestern society. This fundamental set of lifeways probably parallels
responses that developed in other regions of the world, reflecting a
common human reaction to living in a social group within the constraints of simple agricultural production and systematic food gathering. I use the descriptive term "simple agriculturalists" to identify the

peoples who were part of this phenomenon, which appears in almost every temperate part of the world and has had remarkable longevity in most places. The Indians of the Southwest experimented with this life-way and created their own unique and long-lasting version of it. What makes the simple agriculturalist lifeway characteristically Southwestern is the specific adaptations the people in this region developed in order to better their lives and coexist.

In some parts of the world where the environment was especially favorable, simple agriculturalists aggregated into villages that provided the foundation for larger communities and long-lasting state societies, such as those in the Near East, the Mediterranean, and Mesoamerica (see Redman 1978; Stark 1986). In other regions, such as the American Southwest, village agricultural life remained the dominant social form, with periodic but short-lived developments of greater political complex-ity that ultimately dissolved, returning the citizenry to their former village lifeways.

What are the characteristics of this persistent lifestyle as it existed in the American Southwest? Although I will describe them in greater detail in subsequent chapters, the essential features are an easily manageable group size, a reliance on a diversity of food acquisition activities, a will-ingness to relocate settlements after short periods of time, and a cultural resilience that comes from creativity, experimentation, and strong inter-personal social ties that often transcend a single settlement (Adams 1978; Redman 1992). A final characteristic that we believe may have existed at Shoofly Village was the ability to integrate diverse, possibly ethnic, groups. The size and form of the actual communities that simple agri-culturalists built and inhabited certainly varied from region to region, even within the Southwest. Around the Payson-Star Valley area, the simple agricultural lifeway existed in three fundamentally different com-munity forms—household, hamlet, and village. According to archae-ological research in this area, households and hamlets appear to be the most enduring and resilient settlement forms, while the village, at least in the Payson region, was far more transitory. Chapters 4, 5, 6, and 7 present the archaeological evidence concerning each of these community forms and provide insights into their functions and organization.

By arguing that the simple agriculturalist social phenomenon and the three community forms it assumed in the Payson area have some universal relevance, I do not mean that they were uniformly present in all regions of the world, let alone in different parts of the Southwest. What I do maintain is that within the great diversity of small-scale societies across the world, there are important shared elements that can be found in many widely separated cases, elements that should form the basis of a more sophisticated understanding of the common human condition today and in the past.

This book is devoted to the archaeological discovery and interpretation of one of these simple agricultural societies: the prehistoric people who inhabited the area below the Tonto section of the Mogollon Rim surrounding the modern town of Payson, Arizona. Because these people did not have an easily characterized, repeatedly exhibited, set of material cultural traits, nor a high-profile period of great economic and cultural florescence, they have been slighted by scholars and researchers whose omission denies them a distinct identity and contribution. They remain a people without a name of their own, a people that archaeologists characterized as lacking a culture in their own right. It is this situation that is most disconcerting. The very qualities of these people that have frustrated many scholars are at the heart of their importance for our understanding of the past: their enduring adaptive flexibility. Perhaps more than any other agriculturalists of the Southwest, the people under the Tonto Rim integrated a diversity of lifestyles with creativity. They are clearly people who moved about, coming in contact with outsiders and adopting or rejecting a vast array of ideas and innovations. They tried and incorporated a variety of external innovations, including domesticated plants, a settled way of life, surface masonry, contiguous architecture, and advanced pottery technologies, into a regional lifeway of their own. Knowledge of how these people worked with what was available to them could become the keystone of a new understanding of prehistoric Southwestern society and perhaps, by extension, world society.

3 □ □ □ Nature Sets the Stage

To best understand the prehistoric lifeways of the people of Shoofly Village and other settlements under the Tonto Rim, it is necessary to describe the natural environment within which they lived. First I examine the general region and then look more closely at the immediate vicinity of Shoofly Village and the other sites that are discussed in this volume.

Arizona is one of the most topographically varied and scenic areas in North America, containing within its boundaries extensive forests, vast deserts, surprisingly numerous riparian zones, and even a small area of alpine tundra (see Lowe 1964). Accompanying the diversity of geography and climate is a variety of rich biotic communities. These natural resources—land, climate, flora, and fauna—set the stage for the human occupation of the area. They were the raw materials for shelter and subsistence, and they set constraints on what was possible to achieve, even through human ingenuity. Arizona contains rich natural resources that its early inhabitants developed and utilized in many effective ways.

In order to understand the lifeways developed by the people under the Tonto Rim, it is important to have a general knowledge of the environmental factors that conditioned life in central Arizona as well as a more detailed familiarity with the immediate region. Shoofly Village is situated midway between the southern escarpment of the Colorado Plateau and the northernmost reaches of the Sonoran desert in the Tonto Basin and Verde River Valley. This intermediate zone of hills, mesa tops, and small river valleys was home to the prehistoric people of Shoofly Village and their neighbors. The area surrounding the modern towns of Payson and Star Valley are the focus of the archaeological investigations reported here (Fig. 3.1). Each town has grown up in a small valley surrounded by hills and mesas. Together they form a convenient unit for research into and interpretation of the past.

Regional Environmental Context

CLIMATIC ZONES

In order to discuss Arizona's complex environment, scientists have found it useful to divide the state into several sections. The geographic subdivisions used in Figure 3.1 were devised by climatologist William Sellers (Sellers et al. 1985) and have served as a reference point for many subsequent studies. The natural area in which Shoofly Village was built is referred to as the "central" section, which reflects both its geographic location in the state and the transitional character of its topography positioned between the upland plateaus to the northeast and the lowland deserts to the southwest.

Some of the most rugged terrain in Arizona lies in the central section, which is composed of a series of stream-fed basins isolated from one another by mountain ranges. This has given rise to the name "basin and range," which geographers use for this region. Intermittent streams are abundant but the only permanent rivers are the Verde, Salt, and Gila. The East Verde River, a tributary of the Verde River, and Tonto Creek, which flows into the Salt River, frame the Payson-Star Valley area that is the focus of this book. Chaparral and oak, juniper, and pinyon woodlands cover most of the region, while ponderosa forests grow at some of the higher elevations and desert flora in the lower canyons.

Immediately to the northeast is the Colorado Plateau with elevations between 6,000 and 8,000 ft and a steep escarpment called the Mogollon

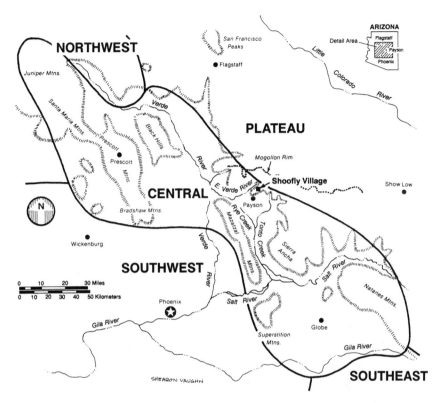

3.1   Climatic sections of central Arizona. (Adapted from Sellers 1964.)

Rim that separates it from the central section. Ponderosa pine forests
and stands of pinyon and juniper are the characteristic vegetation types
of the plateau. A few alpine meadows occur at the highest elevation
among the scattered mountain ranges, while dispersed patches of chaparral and oak woodlands are present at some of the lower elevations.

To the southwest is the driest and most typically desert area of Arizona. This section is characterized by flat desert plains crisscrossed by
numerous arroyos that are separated from one another by low craggy
hills. The minimal rainfall and limited distribution of ground water has
always presented a major problem for the inhabitants of this region.
The Salt and Gila rivers and a number of smaller rivers that feed into
their systems offer the most reliable sources of water.

PRECIPITATION

One of the distinguishing characteristics of the central section of the state is its relatively heavy precipitation compared with that in the surrounding areas. Even the lower, more desert-appearing locations on the edge of the central section, which are monitored by the Roosevelt and Reno weather stations in the Tonto Basin, receive twice as much rain as the station at Mesa, only 40 mi away but in the Sonoran Desert. The weather station at Payson has recorded an average annual precipitation of 21.5 in, and the nearby station at Tonto Natural Bridge has recorded 24.2 in (Sellers and Hill 1974). Abundant rain is particularly desirable for simple agriculture because it provides both direct moisture for crops during the summer growing season and sufficient water to fill the drainage catchments of the region.

Precipitation across Arizona is dominated by two distinct weather patterns: from a southerly direction during the summer and from the north and west in the winter. Summer precipitation comes from storms that are primarily convectional in nature, often intense, and characteristically local rather than widespread (Lowe 1964:8). This pattern results from moist tropical air moving into the state from the Gulf of Mexico or the Gulf of California and then passing over strongly heated mountainous terrain, which causes the moist air to rise rapidly, cool, and condense. Nowhere is this truer than in the Payson-Star Valley area where the steep escarpment of the Mogollon Rim blocks the passage of air masses in their flow north, causing as much or more precipitation to fall in this area than in any other part of the state. Summer rainfall occurs from mid-May to mid-October, although May and June are sometimes rainless. The summer rains (referred to locally as monsoons) begin abruptly in early July, breaking the spring-summer drought.

Winter precipitation is associated with westerly winds that bring polar Pacific air moisture onto the North American continent across the Washington, Oregon, or California coasts, sometimes traveling as far inland as Arizona. When the storms reach Arizona, the ground is cooler than it is in the summer, which slows the upslope movement of the air mass and leads to widespread cloudiness and relatively gentle rainstorms that cover a wide area. In the Payson area three-fourths of the winter precipitation falls as rain, with only 25 in of snow in a normal year. Of special interest to us here is the localized pattern of heavier rainfall to the east of Payson and lighter rainfall to the west during the summer.

Interestingly, on average, almost half of Arizona's annual precipitation falls during each of the two rainy seasons. Winter precipitation is decidedly more variable from year to year than summer rainfall, both in its amount and in its time of occurrence. But it is the consistent beginning date and amount of summer precipitation that is more important when considering the suitability of the region for agriculture. The major drawback of the summer rains is that they fall unevenly across the landscape in scattered dense storms. This is somewhat mitigated in the Payson-Star Valley area by the high escarpment of the Mogollon Rim, which focuses numerous storms in the area directly south of the rim.

TEMPERATURE

The temperature, which varies widely across Arizona, is largely correlated with elevation as well as with latitude (Sellers and Hill 1974). The low deserts of the southwestern section have average July temperatures of 95F and many days with readings over 100F. In January, temperatures average 55F with few frosts, and daytime temperatures frequently reach into the seventies. In contrast to these warm locations, the highest elevations in the state have average July temperatures of 55F and average January temperatures in the low twenties.

The central section's climate is temperate. In July average temperatures at Payson are 74F, while in January they are 36F. This reflects the very pleasant summer and winter temperatures of the area. Normal summer days have highs in the eighties and lows during the night in the fifties. In the dry months of May and June this diurnal temperature variation often spans 40 degrees or more. The winters are also quite mild with normal daytime temperatures reaching into the fifties and often as high as 70F. During the night the temperature often drops below freezing, but it is extremely rare for temperatures to go below 0F. These moderate temperatures contrast with the extreme summer heat of the neighboring lowlands to the south and the winter cold of the highlands to the north. It is not unusual for the Payson area to be 20

Table 3.1   Climatological Data for Payson Region. (Adapted from Miller 1990).

Years	Frost- Free Days	Annual Rainfall	% Rain Apr–Sept	% Rain Oct–Mar
1949–1959	169	21.0 in	51	49
1960–1969	164	19.2 in	48	52
1970–1979	156	20.6 in	46	54
1980–1984	150	25.9 in	43	57

degrees cooler on a summer day than Phoenix and 15 degrees warmer on a winter day than nearby areas above the Mogollon Rim.

The moderate temperatures were beneficial for simple agriculture. The mild climate provided a long, frost-free growing season for crops and an environment for humans that required minimal protection from temperature extremes. Agronomists have argued that traditional maize agriculture would need about 110 frost-free days, and that areas with more than 15 in of rain would be adequate for dry (rainfall alone) farming (see Snow 1991 and Wills 1988 for a discussion of these requirements). As can be seen from Table 3.1, the Payson-Star Valley region not only exceeds these minimum requirements, but it does so by a substantial amount and in a consistent year-after-year manner. Overall, the climate of this region is favorable for simple agriculture and is hospitable to human settlement.

LIFE-ZONE

The central section of Arizona is part of what ecologists have called the Upper Sonoran life-zone. This zone includes several plant communities that are generally associated with specific elevations (Figs. 3.2–3.3). Of particular importance for studying the prehistory of the Payson-Star Valley area are the interior chaparral, conifer woodland, and deciduous (riparian) woodland communities (Lowe 1964).

The interior chaparral community occurs broadly across the central section, usually at elevations between 4,000 and 6,000 ft, particularly in the foothills below the Mogollon Rim. The area is characterized by dense shrub growth, usually closed, of fairly uniform height between 3 and 7 ft, and broken by an occasional tall shrub or short tree. The

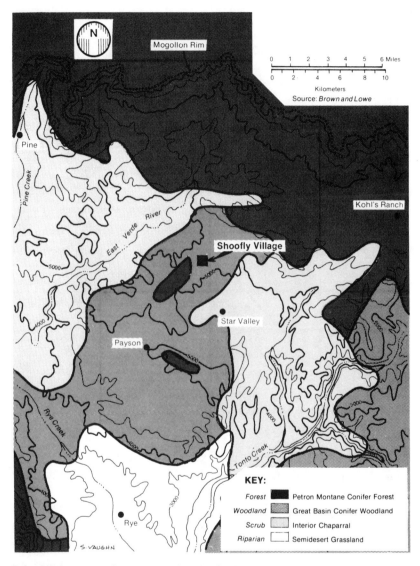

3.2   Major vegetation communities in the Payson region.

dominant plants are generally tough-leaved evergreen shrubs, such as scrub oak (*Quercus turbinella*) and manzanita (*Arctostaphylos pungens; A. pringlei*). Grasses are scarce in the areas of closed chaparral but are more abundant in open chaparral, especially following fires (Lowe 1964:50).

Biotic Communities
in the Shoofly Region

From *Brown and Lowe*

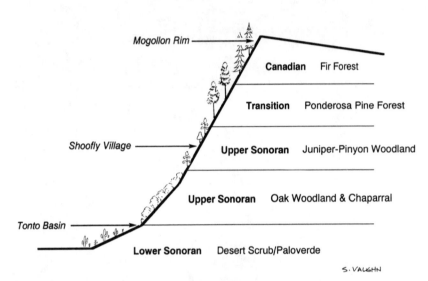

3.3   Elevation gradation of major vegetation communities in the Payson region. (Adapted from Brown and Lowe 1980.)

Early cattle ranchers burned open chaparral areas to clear land for range, and prehistoric farmers may have used fire to prepare an area for maize cultivation.

The conifer woodland community consists largely of juniper and pinyon, often in an "open" grassland type of arrangement. In terms of plant diversity, this community is relatively simple, with sometimes almost pure stands of junipers below a 6,000-foot elevation and pinyons above that level. Juniper species outnumber pinyon species, with the most common being Utah juniper (*Juniperus osteosperma*) followed by alligator juniper (*Juniperus deppeana*) and one-seeded juniper (*Juniperus monosperma*). Colorado pinyon (*Pinus edulis*) and Emory oak (*Quercus emoryi*) are also important components of the woodland zone. The open configuration of the juniper-pinyon woodland encourages the growth of small shrubs and grasses. This would also have made the area suitable for agriculture with minimal modification.

Today, we find scattered stands of ponderosa pine (*Pinus ponderosa*) from Payson east through Star Valley at elevations as low as 4,900 ft. Ponderosa pine, which is the dominant tree of the transitional life-zone above the Mogollon Rim and is not a characteristic member of the upper Sonoran life-zone, is found more frequently in the montane conifer forest zone. I suspect that these ponderosas are relatively recent entries into the lower areas, perhaps arriving after the area had been logged or burned by recent settlers. Our archaeological evidence documents that the predominant tree used prehistorically was juniper, with virtually no ponderosa present.

The deciduous or riparian woodland is the final biotic community of the region. As its name implies, it is found along streams, rivers, and floodplains and, hence, it occurs in relatively narrow bands that are not visible on Figure 3.2. The dominant trees are cottonwood (*Populus fremontii*), willow (*Salix*), sycamore (*Platanus wrightii*), and walnut (*Juglans major*). At one time riparian woodlands occurred throughout the region, but today much of the area is occupied by modern towns, e.g., Payson and Star Valley, so that the habitats have been severely altered, making archaeological investigation difficult. Nevertheless, it is possible to observe this plant community at the margins of these towns and outside their boundaries along streams where small floodplains have developed. It is likely that this community was an important resource zone for the prehistoric inhabitants of the region but, because of modern residential growth, it is underrepresented in our investigations and its contribution is hard to assess.

The diverse topography of the general Payson-Star Valley area provided natural habitats for a variety of fauna (Eshbaugh 1988). Among the larger mammals were mule deer (*Odocoileus hemionus*), antelope (*Antilocapra americana*), bighorn sheep (*Ovis canadensis*), javelina (*Tayassu tajacu*), mountain lion (*Felis concolor*), black bear (*Ursus americanus*), coyote (*Canis latrans*), and gray wolf (*Canis lupus*). Among the smaller mammals were jackrabbits, cottontails, squirrels, chipmunks, gophers, rats, mice, porcupines, skunks, and badgers. In addition, it is believed that permanent streams such as the East Verde River and Tonto Creek would have supported a variety of fish, amphibians, and reptiles.

Beyond that, the Payson area is home to numerous bird species and a temporary stopover for migratory fowl.

Local Environmental Context

GEOLOGY

The Payson-Star Valley region is characterized by rugged terrain containing low mountains, mesas, ridges, and sediment-filled basins (Burton 1991). The main geological deposits consist of a lower stratum of Precambrian rocks overlain by thick sequences of Paleozoic sediments with local covers of Tertiary basalts and Quaternary alluvium (Fig. 3.4). The Paleozoic rocks consist of sequences of nearly flat-lying sedimentary rocks, separated from the underlying Precambrian rocks by an eroded surface known as the Great Unconformity because rock strata once present eroded away before the Paleozoic sediment was deposited. The sites we have investigated near Payson, including Shoofly Village, lie above the Great Unconformity, while those in Star Valley lie below it. The substratum for Houston Mesa where Shoofly is located is made up of Payson Granite, which is not exposed near the site but granitic rubble from it is present. The most abundant rocks visible in the immediate vicinity of Shoofly are derived from the Tapeats Sandstone and Tertiary Basalt strata. Both types of rock were used as building material and are important in local soil formation. The intervening layers of limestone have largely eroded, except where exposures have been protected by caprocks to the north and south of Shoofly. These deposits were quite important to the prehistoric inhabitants because they contained abundant chert and chalcedony nodules that were used as the raw material for stone tools.

The Star Valley sites are located well below the Great Unconformity with the Payson Granite appearing as the local bedrock. Tapeats Sandstone boulders and chert nodules derived from the Paleozoic limestones are abundant components of the alluvium along Houston Creek, a short distance from many of the sites we investigated.

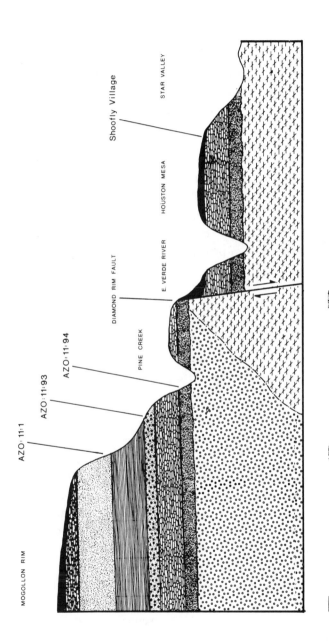

3.4   Idealized geological cross-section from Shoofly Village to the Mogollon Rim. (From Burton 1991.)

SOILS

The soils of Payson and Star Valley are described as cool, subhumid soils and are less agriculturally fertile than the warm, semiarid soils of the recent and deep alluvium of the Tonto Basin to the south (Adams 1968). The soils in Payson and Star Valley are shallow, often mixed with gravel or sandy loam, and rock outcrops cover substantial areas of the surface.

Of the various localities within this region, the alluvium-filled basins, which we refer to as the creek zone (see Lindauer 1991c), have the best soils, rated as "good" for agriculture (Fig. 3.5). Even in the immediate Payson area where Green Valley (the largest basin in our study area) is located, less than 9 percent of the soils have this high rating. In the area of low hills and ridges surrounding the alluvial basins, the shallow, coarser soils of primarily granitic origin are dominant. The permeability of these soils is rapid and the topsoil is rated as "poor" for agriculture. Although soil fertility is low in this part of the upland zone, it still is possible to cultivate crops. The mesas, especially Houston and Birch, form the other major division of the upland zone. They have slowly permeable subsoils with textures that range between clay loam to stony clay loam. Soil fertility is rated as "poor to fair," which, although not great, is somewhat better than the other sections of the upland zone.

TRANSPORTATION

The rugged topography of the entire region makes travel across it relatively difficult (Fig. 3.6). Within individual basins and across some of the major mesas, however, movement is quite easy. The size of these areas is small, though, and to move from one feature to the next it becomes necessary to traverse low hills or canyons formed by one of the many intermittent streams. Although the Green Valley arm of the Payson Basin is enclosed by steep cliffs and slopes on three sides, it is relatively easy to move to the north up onto Houston or Birch mesas following the course of the modern highway. To the west, the terrain becomes quite rugged and travel is difficult. It is somewhat easier to go to the south or east by traversing a series of low hills and ridges in order to reach Round Valley to the south or Star Valley to the east. In fact, the

3.5   View of the valley bottom in the creek zone just west of Payson.

general configuration of the region's topography as seen in Figure 3.6 forms an amphitheater, with highlands to the north and rough topography to the west and eventually to the east. This configuration would tend to funnel the movement of people to the south, as we hypothesize happened in prehistory.

Starting from Shoofly Village, movement in all four directions is relatively easy. Travel to Star Valley is easier on foot than it would appear from the circuitous route that paved roads now follow. In general, it is relatively easy to move north-south through the basins or over the upland flat areas in order to reach the escarpment of the Mogollon Rim. This avoids the need to cross the many canyons formed by streams and arroyos. The streams themselves offer only relatively short routes for travel because most of them pass periodically through narrow gulches on their way south.

Use of the Environment during Historic Times

To gain some perspective on the way people may have perceived the Payson-Star Valley environment during prehistoric times, it is helpful

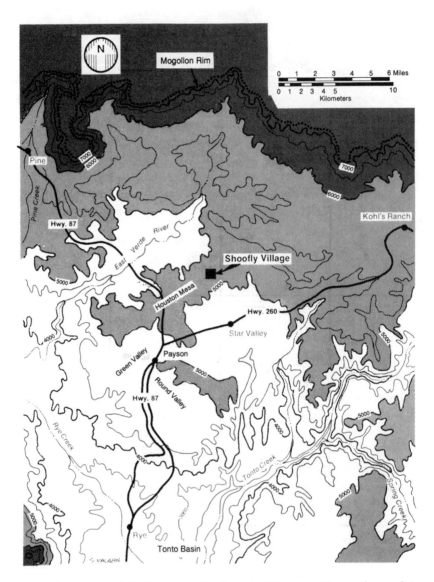

3.6   Topography of the Payson region from the Mogollon Rim on the north to
the Tonto Basin on the south.

to review what is known about its use during the historic period. For this information I have relied heavily on a report written by Steven James (1991) and a volume compiled by the Northern Gila County Historical Society (1984).

Immediately before the entry of Anglo settlers into the area in the 1870s, Payson and its environs were inhabited by the Southern Tonto Apaches (Basso 1983; Buskirk 1949; McGuire 1980). This Apache group was composed of seven bands, one of which resided in the area around Payson, Green Valley, Round Valley, and Star Valley (Buskirk 1986; Goodwin 1942; James 1991). The Southern Tonto Apaches themselves were one of five groups that composed the Western Apache, an Athapaskan-speaking nation that occupied much of eastern Arizona. The Western Apache depended on a variety of subsistence strategies, including hunting, gathering, farming, and raiding (Buskirk 1949, 1986). The Southeastern Yavapai, a Yuman-speaking group, are also known to have occupied this general area during the nineteenth century, although it appears that their range was restricted to west of Payson (Gifford 1936). The Yavapais had a lifeway similar to that of the Western Apache, and consequently their archaeological remains are difficult to distinguish from those of Western Apache people.

Both groups appear to have moved seasonally to exploit ripening wild plant foods (Macnider and Effland 1989). Crops also were planted in particularly moist locations in the late spring, and groups returned to these places in the early fall to harvest the crops that had matured. Both groups relied heavily on roasted agave as a staple, and we know that they hunted and ate deer, elk, and antelope (Buskirk 1949). From ethnographic accounts we learn that most of their daily subsistence routines were carried out by gender specific task groups, with males responsible for hunting and women for plant gathering. Groups would occasionally come together in base camps for substantial periods of time when sufficient local resources were available.

The date of the entry of the Western Apache and/or Yavapai groups into the Payson-Star Valley area is a subject of active inquiry, without convincing conclusions. One point that appears to be clear is that these groups did not occupy the area during prehistory. In fact, there seems to be a very low population density, if any permanent occupation at all, in the Payson-Star Valley area from A.D. 1400 to the entry of Western

Apache/Yavapai peoples in proto-historic times. Later in this volume, I will suggest some reasons for the virtual abandonment of this region by A.D. 1400. The current consensus on the reoccupation of central Arizona, including the Payson-Star Valley area, is that the Yavapais probably inhabited the Verde River Valley and the Apaches moved from the Colorado Plateau south across the Mogollon Rim by about A.D. 1600. In our own archaeological investigations we have found several sites with evidence of Apache/Yavapai use, and several other groups working in the region have as well (Bruder and Ciolek-Torrello 1987; Gregory 1991b; Hohmann and Redman 1988; Huckell 1978; Redman and Hohmann 1986). None of the sites has been very substantial; rather, they contain lightly built shelters, roasting pits, and a few artifacts that allow us to identify them as Apache/Yavapai. One radiocarbon date derived from a site we excavated, Scorpion Rock Ruin, indicated the possibility that the Payson area was occupied in the sixteenth-century, but another radiocarbon determination from the same site, as well as several from other expeditions, suggests that the early date is an anomaly and that Apache/Yavapai settlement in the region began only in the seventeenth or even eighteenth century.

Anglo settlers also entered the Payson region relatively late—in the mid-nineteenth century. Several factors contributed to this situation: first, the area lacked high-grade gold or silver deposits; second, it was difficult to reach from the north due to the Mogollon Rim; and third, it was considered unsafe for homesteading until the mid-1860s when, after the Civil War, soldiers became available to protect settlers. The first military activity in the area took the form of punitive expeditions against the Apaches led by King S. Woolsey in 1864 (James 1991). These took Woolsey to the vicinity of the modern towns of Miami and Strawberry, and gave him an opportunity to name Tonto Creek and the East Verde River. Several military camps were established along the banks of the Verde River to provide a permanent base to handle the Indian conflicts. Camp Lincoln, later renamed Camp Verde, and Camp McDowell to the south, just east of what would later become Phoenix, were established in 1865. General Crook, who had taken command of the Arizona posts, launched several military campaigns against the Tonto Apaches and Yavapais in 1872 and 1873. These campaigns ultimately led to the resettlement of many Apaches on a

reservation near Camp Verde and their later relocation to the San
Carlos Reservation in 1875 (James 1991). With that, the region around
Payson was opened to white settlement. Andrew and Samuel Houston
purchased land in 1876 in what they were later to name Star Valley, and
in 1878 they brought in 300 head of Durham cattle from California to
graze in Star Valley and on Houston Mesa in the vicinity of the ruins of
Shoofly Village.

Mining attracted other settlers to the region around Payson at about
the same time as ranching, but the development of mines was never
very successful in the area (James 1991). In 1876 William Burch and
John Hood settled in present-day Payson, which then was known as
Green Valley, in order to work the Golden Waif Mine, the first recorded
mine in the area. A short-lived mining camp called Marysville was
founded in 1880 a few miles west of what would become Payson. The
settlement lasted for about three years and had as many as 100 inhabitants at its peak.

A formal town site, then named Union Park, was surveyed in 1882
by John Hise and James Callahan. When a U.S. Post Office was
opened in 1884, the postmaster changed the name of Union Park to
Payson in honor of the Congressional chairman of the Post Office who
had been responsible for his appointment (Granger 1960:110).

In the late nineteenth and early twentieth centuries, Payson grew
slowly. In 1887, an episode that affected the lives of many Paysonites
began: a feud between two ranching families in nearby Pleasant Valley
that lasted for five years. It has been referred to as the Pleasant Valley
War and was romanticized in the writings of Zane Grey and others.
Altogether, 29 men lost their lives in the conflict.

A major event that contributed to the growth of Payson was the
construction of Roosevelt Dam to the south. This was the first project of
the newly created U.S. Reclamation Service and it drew labor and
supplies from Payson as well as from other neighboring communities.
Construction lasted from 1905 to 1911. Partially as a result of this
project, the Tonto Forest Reserve (now the U.S. Department of Agriculture's Tonto National Forest) was established in 1905 to help protect
the watershed above Roosevelt Dam. It has been estimated that in 1900
there were 20 times the number of cattle on range than there are today
(Northern Gila County Historical Society 1984). Poor market condi-

tions combined with droughts, however, seriously hurt the ranchers. Heavy rains subsequently caused major erosion throughout the area, intensifying the need for serious range management (Macnider and Effland 1989). Much of the land surrounding Payson and all of the land on which we have conducted our excavations was ultimately included in the Tonto National Forest and since then has been subject to Federal regulation. It is reasonable to conclude that during the past century of Anglo occupation there has been substantial erosion of the already fragile soils due to overgrazing and logging activities.

4 □ The Payson-Star Valley
□ Settlement System
□

In *Under the Tonto Rim*, Zane Grey referred to the territory around Payson as the "backwoods," a region of particularly dense plant and wild animal life. He also meant that the area was hard to travel in because of the streams and arroyos that dissected it. Grey came to the Payson area as a hunter and eventually spent much productive time there. As it was for Zane Grey, so it may have been for the prehistoric Indians.

Although movement through much of the territory is difficult, nestled within this rough countryside are several relatively large basins that are well-watered and support natural grasslands. The Payson Basin with its extension to the west and the smaller Star Valley Basin to the east would have been particularly suitable for early agriculturalists. The low hills surrounding these basins could have served as lookouts, and the arroyos and creeks that periodically fill with water could have provided supplemental water to scattered farm plots. This would have been attractive to early farmers who were organized in small groups, as well as to hunters and gatherers. The area to the north of Star Valley and Payson is dominated by Houston and Birch mesas (Fig. 4.1). The mesa tops offer open country settings dissected by a few arroyos and

4.1   View of upland zone topography seen from Deer Jaw Ruin towards
Risser Ranch Ruins where modern houses have been built.

semipermanent streams. These areas would provide reasonably good
hunting opportunities and certain locations would be favorable for simple agriculture. My own inference is that successful occupation of the
mesa-top locations required a more organized approach to farming and
settlement construction than was necessary in the basins.

Chronology of Prehistoric Settlement

Although this entire region is inadequately described in the culture
histories of the Southwest, a summary of current thinking on the local
chronology is shown in Table 4.1 (Hohmann and Redman 1988; Lindauer, Bradley, and Redman 1991; Macnider and Effland 1989; Redman and Hohmann 1986; Stafford 1979, Wood 1985).

Summaries of regional settlement are usually based on a variety of
sources of information and represent the best reconstruction of the
essential characteristics and relative antiquity of communities in the

Table 4.1 Chart of Chronological Phases for the Prehistoric Cultures of the Payson Region. (Adapted from Redman and Hohmann 1986:8.)

UNNAMED PALEOINDIAN: ca. Clovis
The Silktassel site is reported as a Clovis manifestation (Huckell 1978).

UNNAMED ARCHAIC: ca. 8000 B.C.-A.D. 700
Local manifestation of Chiricahua/Armargosa Archaic. Base camps along drainages, task and travel camps in uplands, isolated projectile points. One site tested, but little information available.

UNION PARK: ca. A.D. 700-1000
Introduction of Hohokam patterns by direct colonization or from indigenous associations with Hohokam colonies in Upper Tonto Basin/East Verde Valley. Pithouse villages expected in main valleys.

STAR VALLEY: ca. A.D. 1000-1150
Basically a rural adaptation of both Hohokam patterns introduced earlier and surface architecture settlements. Household communities and hamlets in creek zone. Early phases of villages established now.

PAYSON: ca. A.D. 1150-1300
Village farming site complexes with large compound centers (e.g., Shoofly Village, Risser Ranch, Round Valley) and smaller compound/hamlets (up to 30 rooms) and extensive rural agricultural population in household size communities with abundant runoff control facilities. Risser Ranch Ruin partially excavated by Scottsdale Community College and Arizona Archaeological Society. Shoofly Village investigated by ASU.

region. The reader should recognize that these reconstructions evolve and change as new information is recovered in the field and as new methods of analysis and interpretation of extant data are applied. One of the first problems is whether we, as archaeologists, have discovered a representative collection of settlements from all time periods. In many parts of the world, as in the Payson area, it is especially difficult to develop a detailed reconstruction for the earlier time periods because there are usually only a few sites covering a span of hundreds or even thousands of years. Hence, it is important to realize that these are very hypothetical statements, more conjectural than factual, to be used only as a guide to what may have happened. By A.D. 1000 in the Payson area, we are on firmer ground with hundreds of sites dated to the following centuries. Interestingly, our information becomes scarce once again for the late prehistoric period, probably reflecting both a decreasing population and the more lightly built settlements present at that time.

The second difficulty in developing regional summaries is how well we are able to date the archaeological settlements that are discovered. The two primary means for assigning a date to a site are the presence of distinctive artifacts or features that have been dated in other regions (cross-dating) and the direct dating of archaeological material through radiocarbon analysis or archaeomagnetic measurement (absolute dating). Radiocarbon dating is a method that estimates the age of carbonized wood or other organic material based on the steady decay of a naturally occurring radioactive isotope of carbon. Appendix 1 summarizes all of the radiocarbon dates derived from our project. A variety of contextual and contamination problems can skew these dates so that in many cases they do not represent the true age, but in the majority of cases they are our best means of determining the age of a site (see Lindauer 1991b for a fuller discussion). Archaeomagnetic measurement is based on the principle that iron particles found in soil will reorient themselves toward magnetic north when the soil they are in is burned. Hence, in the case of a hearth where the soil is fixed in place, it is possible to measure the orientation of magnetic north at the time the soil was last burned. Because the movements of magnetic north are known, scientists are able to estimate the age of a hearth based on its magnetic properties (Eghimy and McGuire 1988). Appendix 2 contains the archaeomagnetic dates from our project. A limiting factor in the use of both techniques is that samples must come from good contexts in excavated sites. Material from survey sites usually cannot be analyzed, and not even all excavated sites provide appropriate samples.

By contrast, cross-dating can be done on distinctive artifacts and features from both survey and excavated sites, but the precision of the technique is often not as good (see discussion in Chapter 8). Unfortunately, nearly all of the material from the Payson sites was locally made, and, consequently, it failed to provide strong links to better dated regions. In general, the cross-dating of sites yields only very broad time ranges whose precision can be improved only with continued excavation and absolute dating of large numbers of samples from the region.

There is little evidence of human settlement in the Payson-Star Valley region before A.D. 800, but the area appears to have served periodically as a resource zone for small groups of hunters and gatherers. These people might have traveled north from the Tonto Basin or south along the Verde River, but they probably did not stay in the Payson-Star Valley area for any length of time. South of present-day Payson along the natural passageway down to the Tonto Basin, researchers have investigated a site with paleoindian material that has been attributed to the Clovis period (Huckell 1978). Although little was learned about the occupants, the evidence from this site does point to some human presence in the region anywhere from 3,000 to 10,000 years ago. In the following period, the Archaic, there appears to have been very little human use of the region. Archaeological surveys have found a few possible hunter-gatherer base camps, and our own project has excavated Horton Rock Shelter, which contained a level attributable to the Archaic period, dating perhaps to some time between A.D. 300 and A.D. 600. This evidence, however, does not point to any substantial settlement in the region. The overall picture is of an open landscape that people occasionally entered to obtain resources and, if they settled there at all, they stayed only for a short period of time.

Archaeological evidence indicates that the area began to be settled around A.D. 850, in what Wood (1985) calls the Union Park phase. In sites from this period, archaeologists have found remains that resemble those of the Hohokam people to the south: Santa Cruz/Sacaton red-on-buff and Gila plain ceramics, slate palettes, worked shell, and pithouses. This evidence suggests either that Hohokam settlements were established in the Payson area or that trade contacts were set up between Payson and Hohokam groups, resulting in the spread of Hohokam features into the area. Although some older Hohokam ceramics are present at Payson sites, the full suite of Hohokam attributes appears only around A.D. 850.

The Union Park phase represents a period of still very low population densities, consisting of scattered hamlets of a few families that settled in the region for limited periods of time, perhaps not even staying year-round. In fact, the settlements were so scattered and the population density so low that it might be more appropriate to consider what was going on as simply exploitation of the territory by individual, unrelated groups, rather than as actual settlement. During the Union Park phase, I see the region as continuing to serve primarily as a resource zone that was periodically exploited by river valley people from the south, and, occasionally, these procurement parties, which consisted of a few families at most, actually settled there. A few small pithouse villages of this phase have been excavated by our project, and others have been recorded during surveys of the region. The use of pithouses characterizes building traditions in many locations during the first millennium A.D. and in itself may not signal a direct Hohokam presence.

Beginning around A.D. 1000, the sparsely populated nature of the Payson region altered radically. It is during what Wood (1985) has called the Star Valley phase (A.D. 1000–1150) and the Payson phase (A.D. 1150–1300) that the region experienced its major population growth. Of 255 prehistoric sites that were identified by Kuang-Ti Li (1988) from records at Tonto National Forest, about 95 percent appear to fit into these periods. The lack of indigenous decorated ceramics makes it very difficult to determine precise time spans for sites within this broad period. With the additional architectural, artifactual, and radiocarbon evidence that we have recovered through our own excavations we are able to put many of our excavated sites into a somewhat finer chronological order, but for the majority of sites that are known only from survey, and for those that yielded little material from excavation, this broad time range must suffice.

Following A.D. 1300, there is evidence once again for very limited settlement in the Payson/Star Valley region. It appears that people moved away and the region reverted to use as a resource zone with practically no settled residents. Several hundred years later, during the sixteenth or seventeenth century, settlement in the Payson area resumed, but at a very low density, characterized by small, widely scattered settlements inhabited by people who were highly mobile.

Characteristic Settlement Types

When the archaeological remains of prehistoric settlements are examined, it often appears as if each site has some unique features and should be considered individually. Clearly, all human communities are distinctive in some way. Although we have spent considerable time in the field and in the next three chapters of this book documenting the distinctive nature of many of the diverse settlements we have discovered, it is also very important to highlight the similarities among the Payson sites. These recurring features or patterns provide us with insights that allow us to generalize about the ordinary prehistoric lifestyle in the region. It is an area characterized by fewer repetitive patterns than archaeologists have discovered elsewhere; nevertheless, repetition dominated the lives of those who lived in Payson during the twelfth century, just as it does today.

In order to generalize about the features of the prehistoric settlement pattern and to present the bulk of our discoveries to the reader, I have identified what I believe are the three basic community forms that existed in the Payson-Star Valley region at its zenith in about A.D. 1200: household communities, hamlets, and villages (Fig. 4.2). These settlement types will be briefly defined and the rationale behind their selection will be discussed. In the next three chapters, I will present detailed examples of each of these settlement types and discuss some of the variability within each type.

Household Communities

More than three-fourths of all sites in the Payson area dating to the Star Valley and Payson phases are composed of one, two, or three structures or have no visible architecture at all (see Chapter 7). Projections suggest that there were more than 1,000 small household sites situated throughout the region. About two-thirds of them have architectural remains on the surface, while the rest consist only of artifact scatters (Abbott 1981). Of these small sites, three-fourths are located on ridge tops or hill slopes, one-fifth on mesa tops, and the remaining few on either basin bottoms or mountain tops (Li 1988:60). The sites with architecture probably served as homes for one or two families or task groups while the rest may have functioned as intermittently occupied camps where specialized activities, such as hunting or collecting food or raw materials, took place. We imagine that a few of these sites were occupied year-round and others intermittently during certain seasons. Rarely is there the substantial buildup of refuse or other material that typically occurs at long-term residential sites. Some structures may have served as field houses where members of a village could stay while tending distant agricultural fields or procuring wild

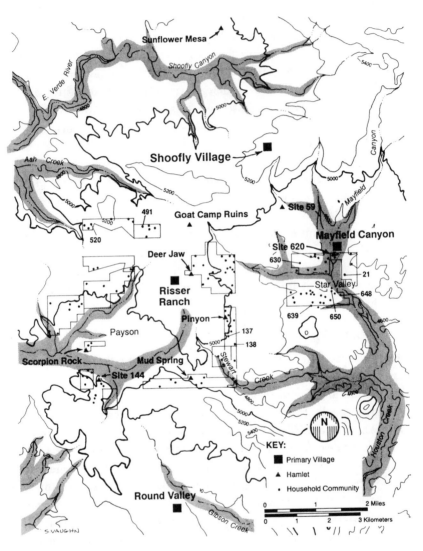

4.2   Map of Payson region with limits of archaeological survey by our project
and location of each archaeological site. The three different community types
discussed in the text are demarcated by different symbols and the rough
boundaries of the creek zone are shaded.

resources. Despite the variety of possible uses, I suspect that many of these small sites actually served as base camps for very small groups and were used for the full range of subsistence activities, albeit for a limited duration of time.

Settlements with between three and six rooms also served as base camps for groups of several families or as camps that were reoccupied several times with new structures being built each time. Li (1988) identified 36 of these sites, which represents about 12 percent of the known prehistoric sites in the region, from the Tonto National Forest records. These settlements were built throughout the region in the same kind of locations as the smaller sites. Close to 90 percent occurred on ridges or hill slopes and the rest were located on mesa tops.

It is likely that many of the three- to six-room sites are, quite simply, reoccupied one- to three-room sites. I postulate that the most elemental social/economic unit in the Payson-Star Valley settlement system consists of two rooms with associated outside features, and, hereafter, I refer to this unit as a "household community." By using the term community, I indicate our belief that many, if not all, of these settlements were economically self-sufficient and autonomous in most respects from their larger neighbors. Needless to say, these small communities would have been tied into larger social networks involving marriage exchange and, probably, procurement of some goods. The surprising point to be highlighted, however, is the degree of autonomy in the daily life of such small settlements.

The physical arrangement of the household community, although on a small scale, does indicate some segregation of activities between structures and in the surrounding outdoor space. The pair of structures that characterize many of the sites often face or are attached to one another. They may house two families or serve as specialized chambers for a single family or task group. Sometimes rebuilding occurred directly on top of the older foundations and sometimes immediately adjacent to the older structure. We also have examples of a series of these small sites spread along a ridge top and separated by anywhere from 10 to 100 meters.

HAMLETS

The next category of settlements ranges in size from six to forty rooms (see Chapter 6). I refer to these population centers as hamlets. I suspect that most hamlets consisted of 10 to 15 rooms that were in actual use at any given time. Once again, as with household communities, some of the hamlets may represent successive communities that were built at the same location. Their room layouts suggest relatively tightly knit communities, often with contiguous rooms arranged around a central courtyard.

The hamlets we have found are located exclusively on hills, ridges, and mesa tops (see Fig. 4.2). Ten have been discovered in the region we are examining. Are these hamlets simply aggregations of several household communities? I think not. Hamlets have more integrated architectural plans, typically with several rooms built around one or more enclosed outdoor spaces. Sometimes this arrangement is repeated within a single site, but the basic unit appears to be five or six rooms and one or two enclosed spaces. I believe that this arrangement is the second primary social/economic unit of the Payson settlement system, housing about 20 to 25 people. These units appear to have rarely existed as isolated communities but rather provided an effective group size where several might aggregate into a single hamlet. The population size of a hamlet, which consisted of between 20 and 100 people, is known from cross-cultural studies to be an appropriate size for an independent community organized along simple kinship lines. I hypothesize that hamlets were inhabited by several related families and that the larger hamlets might be composed of more than one social group or lineage. Such communities could undertake more complex economic tasks than the smaller one- or two-family household community unit, yet they would not be so large that they would require complex social mechanisms to regulate their operation. A common archaeological assumption for settlements of this size would be that they were occupied year-round. Because of the very mobile lifestyle of the people of the Payson-Star Valley region, however, we must examine this assumption on a site-by-site basis.

PRIMARY VILLAGES

Several large settlements of from 50 to 100 rooms represent the primary prehistoric population centers of the Payson-Star Valley region (see Fig. 4.2). The individual rooms in these sites are unusually large by prehistoric standards, and the settlements probably represent even larger population aggregations than the simple room counts indicate (see James 1992). Each settlement probably housed between 200 and 500 people at its peak. The masonry walls represent a substantial energy input and the quantity of refuse accumulation indicates a reasonably long occupation span. From our excavations at Shoofly Village, it is apparent that a range of ceremonial, as well as subsistence, activities were performed there. It is also clear from the Shoofly evidence that the villagers were well-established agriculturalists. Based on these characteristics, I refer to these large settlements as primary villages.

Four primary villages are known, from surveys, to exist in the region. These have been named Shoofly Village, Risser Ranch, Mayfield Canyon, and Round Valley. Most of our information comes from Shoofly Village (see Chapter 5), although some excavation and mapping has been carried out at Risser Ranch as well. I believe that the spatial layout of Shoofly Village can be interpreted as a conglomeration of discrete, distinctive architectural units, each of which looks very much like an individual hamlet site with from six to twenty rooms (Fig. 4.3). Initial surface mapping of Risser Ranch, Mayfield Canyon, and Round Valley reveals the existence of more integrated community plans but also distinct housing units and, possibly, different building styles (Fig. 4.4). Unlike many of the better known Anasazi sites where the overall building plan is uniform and integrated (Lekson 1991), Shoofly Village—and perhaps other villages in the Payson area—appears to retain distinctions in building traditions that might represent formerly separate social groups that joined together in a single community.

The primary villages seem to be evenly spaced over the landscape, each controlling a relatively large productive zone. Risser Ranch, Mayfield Canyon, and Round Valley are each situated on high ground overlooking a valley fed by a semipermanent stream that provided water for a substantial area of agriculturally productive land. Among the primary centers, only Shoofly Village is located in open country on top of a mesa some distance away from streams or valley bottom farmland. The other three village sites also have small outlying compounds that may have been integral parts of their communities. Additionally, Risser Ranch and Round Valley have central core areas that are segmented into several unconnected compounds. To me, these differences

4.3   Photo taken of Shoofly Village Ruins from a small airplane at the
beginning of the project. Ring of trees demarcates the extent of the ruins.
Some lines of wall stones are visible from the air.

in site structure indicate that Shoofly Village filled a somewhat different
role than the other three villages.

The Mayfield Canyon site (AR-03-12-04-22) was surveyed by our
project in conjunction with our excavations of a nearby hamlet, Site
620. Both the Mayfield Canyon Site and Site 620 are located on the
same north-south oriented terrace between Houston Creek and Mayfield Canyon Wash. The relatively broad alluvial areas created by these
intermittent streams provided the residents of both communities, as
well as several other small sites, with easy access to favorable farmland.
Our surface mapping of the Mayfield Canyon site (Fig. 4.4) revealed a
core roomblock of over 20 large rooms with probably another 20
attached to the core or dispersed in small clusters around the core.
Beyond the architectural remains and on the terrace slopes are dense
surface scatters of artifacts indicating the presence of middens.

The artifacts recovered from Mayfield Canyon reflect an inventory
largely similar to that found at most sites in the Payson/Star Valley
area. The vast majority of ceramics consisted of Tonto-Verde plain-

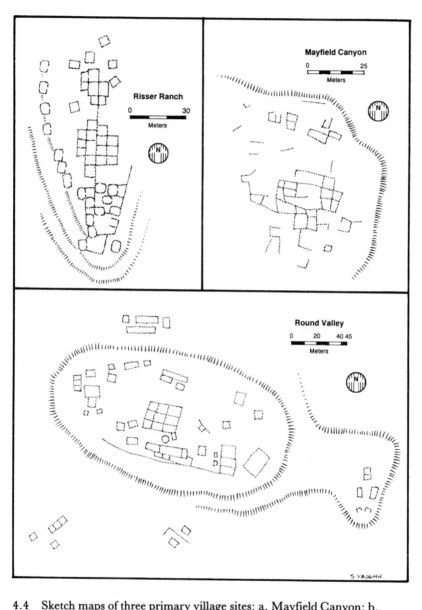

4.4   Sketch maps of three primary village sites: a, Mayfield Canyon; b, Risser Ranch; and c, Round Valley.

wares, but, interestingly, the Verde variety outnumbered the Payson sub-variety that characterizes most other sites we have investigated (see Chapter 8). Among the limited number of decorated ceramics found, Little Colorado White wares, Tusayan wares, and Salado Red were all present, suggesting that the primary occupation was concentrated between A.D. 1200 and A.D.1300. Of great interest was the recovery of four Hohokam buffwares attributed to the Gila Butte and Snaketown phases that date to A.D. 500–850 and a Lino Grey sherd that is of roughly the same date but would have come from the east or north. The presence of these older sherds indicates to us that an earlier site, possibly with pithouses, may exist below the pueblo architecture we have mapped. Given the favorable geographic setting of the Mayfield Canyon site with its nearby arable land, it is not surprising that it was one of the first sites settled in this region and that it remained in use up until the region was largely abandoned.

Risser Ranch (AR-03-12-04-12) is situated on top of a large hill whose summit commands views over the Payson Basin to the west and Star Valley to the east. It appears to have been as large, or perhaps larger, than Shoofly Village, but a modern housing development has obscured much of it. Originally investigated by archaeologists from Scottsdale Community College, the remaining sections of Risser Ranch have been studied in recent years by the Shoofly Chapter of the Arizona Archaeological Society (E. Riggs, personal communication). Surface mapping has recorded a portion of a substantially built roomblock of almost 30 rooms. According to earlier survey notes, it appears that this core roomblock originally was as much as twice this size. Recent research has revealed that outlying rooms covered a much larger area, perhaps 120 m by 50 m, and that many of these rooms appear to be subrectangular. Along the eastern edge of the roomblock there is a substantial wall that may have enclosed much of the settlement, but it does not appear to have been continuous around the entire village as it is at Shoofly Village.

In the core area of Risser Ranch several soundings and two rooms have been excavated by Arizona Archaeological Society members. One room, designated number 8, is particularly interesting for its abundant artifacts and features. The room measured 6 m on each side, making it the largest full-height masonry room we know of in the region. There were two square stone-lined hearths and at least two large postholes that probably held roof supports. Six metates, along with numerous manos, slate knives, deer antlers, ceramics, and lithics, were found. The room obviously was the scene of considerable domestic and, possibly, manufacturing activities. It may have been occupied over a long period of time, possibly even changing function during its lifetime. In contrast to the much smaller rooms that characterize Anasazi pueblos, the very large rooms of the Payson area appear to have had less specialized use, with each one housing a full range of activities. We believe that the outward appearance of Risser Ranch would have been something like that of Shoofly Village, except that the core roomblock was larger and, at least in the recently investigated area, the peripheral rooms were more tightly clustered around the core. The main roomblock was built of massive full-height masonry with at least a portion of it rising two stories high. The excavators believe that room 8 was entered from the roof, since no doorways were found in its walls. Interestingly, the excavators have identified a series of small postholes that they believe represent the remains of an earlier pithouse that underlies room 8. The strategic setting of this site on top of a large hill makes it a logical spot for habitation during all periods of settlement in the Payson region.

The ceramic material from Risser Ranch indicates that it overlapped in time with other Payson-area villages and perhaps continued to be occupied until the end of the thirteenth century, after most people had left the region. This inference stems from the presence of a few sherds of the Pinto Polychrome style that may have originated in the Tonto Basin. It is not clear whether these sherds represent visits to an already abandoned Risser Ranch settlement or whether some portion of the village was still occupied at the time that Pinto Polychrome was brought to the site.

The fourth known village settlement in the region, Round Valley Ruin (AR-03-12-04-106), is located approximately 6 km south of Payson and Risser Ranch. Situated on top of a high hill overlooking a moderately sized valley bottom, the site was explored by archaeologists from the archaeological research center at Gila Pueblo in 1929, but their records on this work have not been found. Tonto National Forest survey records show Round Valley Ruin to be a complex site with a

substantial core roomblock(s) at the summit of the hill and scattered
small compounds around the slopes. Altogether there may have been
from 60 to 80 rooms, possibly making it as large as Shoofly Village or
Risser Ranch. A continuous wall along the south side of the core roomblock indicates that the village may have been at least partially
enclosed. It is also known that a hamlet-size community is located on a
ridge directly across the small valley. The collection of sherds from the
surface of the primary village site includes an array of plainwares, as
well as a limited number of whitewares from the east and north, that
typify the A.D. 1100–1300 period in the Payson-Star Valley region. The
surface collection also includes a few red-on-buff sherds that indicate
contact with earlier Hohokam groups. Several Jeddito black-on-yellow
sherds were found that suggest that people still visited Round Valley in
the fourteenth century and that they had contact with groups in the
Hopi area to the north. The very sketchy picture painted by the evidence we have for Round Valley is of a village similar to Risser Ranch
that consisted of an aggregation of small room clusters grouped around
a main core roomblock in a setting that dominated an area of arable
land.

    Although we are not as confident about the location or number of
hamlets as we are about the more visible primary villages, it appears
that each village may have had one or more hamlets associated with it.
Petrographic analyses of ceramics from some of these sites point to the
possibility that special relationships existed between certain villages and
one or more nearby hamlets (Simon 1988). This is especially important
because, in general, the settlement system in Payson, and in most other
areas of the Southwest, fails to exhibit either interdependence or hierarchical relationships among communities. Although I propose that
most settlements are economically autonomous, and I continue to
believe that a dependency relationship did not exist between the hamlets and small household communities that characterize the Payson
landscape, I do see the possibility of a significant relationship between
the hamlets and primary agricultural villages. This is a subject we will
return to later.

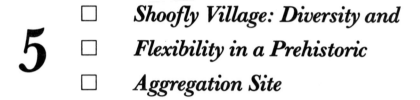

5

☐ *Shoofly Village: Diversity and*
☐ *Flexibility in a Prehistoric*
☐ *Aggregation Site*

The site of Shoofly Village is easily accessible to modern travelers, and
it has been visited intermittently since it was abandoned some 800 years
ago. The casual visitor and archaeologist alike are drawn to the site by
its impressive setting and the visible traces of extensive architecture on
its surface (Fig. 5.1). The site has been known since the first archaeological reconnaissance in the region, and it has been called by more
than one name and given numerous survey numbers. The name Shoofly Village Ruins, derived from the name of a nearby arroyo, was
widely used by local residents; the name was adopted by the ASU team
first in 1975 and then used by our own project. The site has also been
called Houston Mesa Ruins and is listed by that name in the National
Register of Historic Places. The village is situated on the gently sloping
top of a high plateau at about 1600 m (5,240 ft) elevation (Fig. 5.2).
Today, as in prehistoric times, an open juniper woodland with interspersed grass and shrubs surrounds Shoofly Village.

Why did the prehistoric inhabitants of the area choose this particular
location? The answer is not simple. In order to interpret the meaning of
the remains we have found, we as archaeologists make several assump-
tions. One of the most important is that people in the past, as those

53

5.1   Artist's reconstruction of Shoofly Village Ruins. (By Jon Joha.)

today, acted in a rational, economic manner. This means that, in general, their decisions were made in such a way that they would be able to derive the maximum benefit from their livelihoods with the least necessary expenditure of effort. Although there may be specific exceptions to this principle, it serves as a good beginning point for interpreting the past.

The first inhabitants and subsequent immigrants to Shoofly Village were confronted with a number of alternatives on where to locate their settlement. Factors such as safety, access to water, proximity to food and raw materials, and the location of already established communities all must have been considered in their decision making. The site offers a fine position to watch for intruders from the north, west, and south, but if it were located several hundred meters to the east, it would be at the highest point on the mesa with a 360° view (Fig. 5.3). It is not immediately adjacent to a modern spring or along a wash that might have provided easy access to water; the nearest wash is about a kilome-

5.2   View of excavation at Shoofly Village with the Mazatzal Mountains to the southwest in the background.

ter to the north. Furthermore, it does not overlook a cultivatable alluvial valley like the other three primary villages in the region. Our belief is that the availability of building stones and cultivatable land lower down the mesa top convinced the early settlers of Shoofly to establish their community where they did. In addition, some of the soils in the immediate vicinity, especially to the west, are well-developed and hold moisture moderately well (Broderick 1973), with good potential for supporting native vegetation and agricultural plant growth. To the east on the Walnut Flat extension of the mesa there is evidence for an extensive system of check dams that would have been built to enhance the agricultural suitability of the otherwise poor soils of the area.

By the time Shoofly was established, people had been in the region for some time, mainly living in small mobile groups. This had allowed them to acquire a good logistical understanding of the resources available in the area. The fact that Shoofly eventually became one of the largest population aggregates in the region indicates that the potential inhabitants believed this to be a favorable setting. My explanation of the situation is that although Shoofly did not provide the optimum

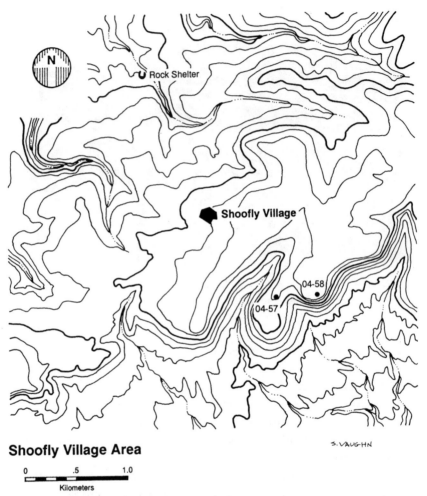

Shoofly Village Area

5.VAUGHN

0   .5   1.0
Kilometers

5.3   Topographic map of the Shoofly Village area, including the closest sites.

setting for any single attribute, it offered a reasonable mixture of all of them: water, farmland, building stones, raw materials for tools, strategic visibility, and a special advantage—isolation from other settlements. I believe that this mixture of features shows, once more, the characteristic response of the groups that settled in central Arizona to maximize their adaptive flexibility, even if it meant not fully capitalizing on any single resource.

The immediate vicinity of Shoofly was sparsely settled. Although the entire region has not been surveyed, our inspection revealed no sites within half a kilometer of the village. Tonto National Forest records indicate that the nearest sites (04-57 and 04-58) are about 1 km to the southeast along the southern escarpment of Houston Mesa (see Fig. 5.3). These are two small household communities with two to four rooms and with very few artifacts exposed on the surface. On the slope below them is a concentration of petroglyphs. Just over 1 km to the north of Shoofly in the upper drainage of Shoofly Wash is a rock shelter with numerous bedrock mortars and several petroglyphs and picto-graphs (Fig. 5.4). These are the only known sites within a 1.5 km radius of Shoofly Village. The low site density is about average for the region, implying that the small outlying communities may be unrelated to the larger site. The sites to the southeast, however, are well placed to command a view over the broad lowlands to the south and to provide lithic raw material from the mesa escarpment. The rock shelter to the north may have been a pinyon nut processing area; today, a higher proportion of pinyon trees are found near it than in the immediate Shoofly area. It also may have been a location for procuring water. At the time of our investigations, the closest known hamlets to Shoofly were Site 04-59, about 2 km to the south; Site 04-35, about 3 km to the east; and Sunflower Mesa Ruin, just over 4 km to the northwest. In 1991 we were fortunate to examine a previously unrecorded hamlet, Goat Camp Ruin (04-968), located about 3 km southwest of Shoofly.

In contrast to the wide spacing of settlements near Shoofly Village, there is a high concentration of settlements and evidence of longer occupations in the zones near the creeks and streams throughout the Payson-Star Valley region. I imagine that, over time, something of a crowding problem developed in the creek zones and on the adjacent ridges near modern-day Payson and Star Valley. The physical layout and the setting of Shoofly indicate to me that its founders were seeking a territory that could be easily defended and was not already occupied by competing groups.

The reasons that the first settlers of Shoofly selected the site provide some interesting insights into possible forces at work in the region. It should be noted that Shoofly Village started as a small settlement and grew by aggregation over a period of a century or more. I believe that

5.4   View of rock shelter north of Shoofly Village. Note bedrock mortar
depressions in front of the shelter and zigzag line on the shelter wall.

the initial rationale behind Shoofly's location was its access to a wide
variety of necessary resources. But because it was situated in an open,
uncrowded environment, it remained attractive to new groups that
subsequently joined the settlement. Its geographic location to the north
of other village settlements and its higher elevation were also important. Although it may be biased by uneven archaeological survey cover-
age, the current evidence indicates that all of the other competing
primary villages in the region were located to the south of Shoofly (i.e.,
Risser Ranch, Mayfield Canyon, and Round Valley). Shoofly's position may have given its inhabitants special access to the resources
directly under the Mogollon Rim and proximity to the route up and
over the rim.

Shoofly's architectural layout also suggests that its residents may
have come from different groups—each with a distinct building tradition. At this point we have hypothesized that the village grew by incor-
porating formerly separate independent groups from different geographic locations and/or from different ethnic or cultural traditions.

Thus, among the questions that I will address in my examination of the remains at Shoofly are: Was the village population composed of distinct groups? What was the basis of their differences? How did the settlement grow? And what kinds of activities were conducted in the different sections of Shoofly?

Strategies for Archaeological Research at Shoofly

The first serious archaeological work at Shoofly consisted of a brief survey, surface collection, and a single test unit excavation by the ASU field school in 1975 (Dittert 1975; Most 1975). Nine years passed, however, before the ASU field school, with the help of the Tonto National Forest, returned to Shoofly in 1984 under my direction. The evidence we sought during the following four field seasons was meant to provide us with an understanding of subsistence methods at the village, the sequence of its settlement, and the kinds of activities that had taken place at the site. The careful unearthing and detailed recording of the materials in an archaeological site are the primary sources of information that archaeologists have for reconstructing the prehistoric past. The objects themselves often tell much of the story, including the types of foods that were eaten, the appearance of early houses, and the nature of prehistoric implements. We have also found that the context in which objects are found and their association with other objects are rich sources of information to help in reconstructing what went on in a settlement hundreds of years ago. Hence, in the excavation of most village sites in the American Southwest, or in almost any other part of the world, archaeologists utilize some basic methods. Among them are careful excavation in order not to excessively damage the material we find, passing the excavated soil through fine mesh screens in order to recover small and broken pieces, and detailed mapping and note taking on the context of the artifacts within the soil. Finally, at sites like Shoofly Village where there is well-preserved architecture, it is important to carefully record the nature of the structures and their artifactual contents in order to aid in reconstructions.

Beyond seeking information on these basic categories, we focused on two specific questions about Shoofly Village and its residents: How did the people at Shoofly interact with those in other regions, and how was society structured in a village of its size. Following the first excavation season, we decided that the question about interregional interaction was not very compelling at Shoofly Village. Intrusive artifacts (ceramics, lithics, shell, and obsidian that came from other locations), although present, were uncommon. In particular, nonlocal decorated ceramics were very rare, and almost all of those found occurred as small fragments. Because of their small size, we hypothesized that many of them were brought to Shoofly as already broken sherds, complicating their usefulness in defining trading networks. The overall paucity of nonlocal artifacts was taken to indicate that Shoofly was not a node in an interregional trading network, or at least not one that consumed a significant portion of the goods passing through. Instead, it appeared as if Shoofly was a somewhat isolated village, with ties primarily to local resources and other local settlements.

The initial impression of the self-sufficiency of Shoofly Village was further confirmed by the examination of the local undecorated ceramics. The investigators (Simon and Burton 1991) found the same minerals present in almost all of the sherds and identified certain inclusions in the clay as coming from nearby Houston Mesa sources. As a result of the lack of evidence for active participation in interregional exchange, our research efforts became more clearly focused on the second issue—understanding Shoofly's community structure.

For field research, we organized the investigation of community structure into three stages (see Redman 1987). Stage I explorations were to monitor the distribution of architectural and artifactual remains across the site. A detailed map was drawn of surface indications of architecture and 35 1 m by 1 m test excavation units were located on the basis of a randomly generated sample (Fig. 5.5). Using this type of statistical procedure ensured that our soundings would be evenly spaced across the entire site, testing both promising and unpromising areas. This produced representative data that allowed us to speculate further about the use of space, the nature of deposition, the degree of preservation, and the density of artifacts and ecofacts. For example, Stage I excavations revealed that just over half of the area inside the compound wall consisted of unroofed courtyards and plazas. Twenty additional test squares were dug outside the compound wall, revealing

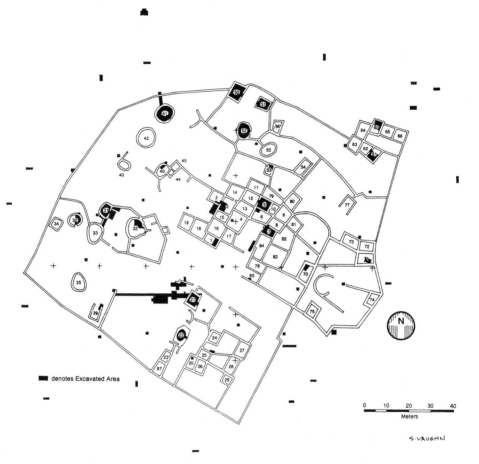

5.5   Map of excavation units and surface indications of walls at Shoofly Village.

the location of scattered refuse deposits in all directions and a single deep midden just outside the wall to the east. Due to the small size of the test units, interpretive information on activities and architecture was suggestive rather than conclusive. More extensive excavations would be necessary to pursue more specific questions.

In order to accurately track where artifacts were discovered, we used a recording system that was based on the number of meters east and north of an arbitrary datum point an artifact was located. This method

was used for all excavation notes, field maps, photograph identifica-
tions, and artifact collections. This allowed us to know exactly where
everything was found on the site. In order to simplify the analysis and
communication, however, we assigned a number between 1 and 100 to
each room at Shoofly, and it is this number that is used in the text of
interpretive volumes such as this one.

The site map generated during 1984 (and improved upon during
later field seasons) revealed what we interpreted as several distinct
groups of associated structures (Fig. 5.6). Moreover, the site did not
appear to have an overall plan, nor was it necessarily constructed during a short period of time. Within one or two sections of the site there
may have been some planning and uniform construction of a particular
block of rooms, but in other areas it appears as if structures were
constructed individually and subsequently connected by low walls or
enclosed later by a compound wall.

We designated a group of contiguously joined rectilinear rooms in
the center of the site as the core roomblock. Surrounding these pueblo-
style core rooms were additional rectangular and curved-wall structures
in an area that we refer to as the periphery. Some of the structures in the
periphery were free-standing while others were joined together into
clusters by low walls that might have enclosed unroofed spaces. Other
structures in the periphery were clearly organized into roomblocks, yet
they were stylistically distinct from the core roomblock. In order to
formulate an excavation plan to continue our investigations we decided
to treat the site as if it were composed of seven separate groups of
structures according to their location on the site and their general construction technique (see Fig. 5.6).

Today, Shoofly Village is dominated by the core roomblock, as it
must have been when it was inhabited (see Figure 5.1). This roomblock
is composed of 27 rectangular rooms and is located at the geographic
center of the settlement. Although we have excavated portions of eight
rooms in the core, the overall layout of the core remains largely a
reconstruction from surface indications. It appears that the roomblock
was built around a small plaza or courtyard opening to the south. Some
of the rooms appear to have had a second story, while surface indications suggest that four of the rooms are extremely large, measuring over
40 m^2 in area. With additional work, we may eventually find that these

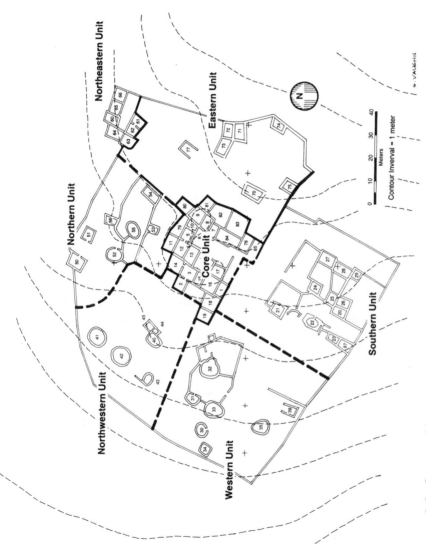

5.6   Seven architectural strata used to structure the excavation strategy at Shoofly Village.

were actually unroofed spaces or were more than one room. The other 23 rooms in the core roomblock average 27 m², still the largest average room size for any section of the site. Moreover, when comparing the core rooms with those in other sections of Shoofly Village, which average about 21 m², or with Anasazi rooms, which average from 10 to 15 m², one gains an appreciation for the unusual effort it took to build the core rooms and the range of activities that might have taken place within them (see James 1992 for a thorough discussion of the implications of these room size differences).

The western, northwestern, and northern units of the village primarily contain freestanding curved-wall structures or small complexes of two or three subrectangular rooms. These areas look less like components of an integrated site than like small, independent rural hamlets placed in close proximity to each other. Most of the rooms have only low preserved walls and modest quantities of rubble, indicating that their masonry walls were never full height or that considerable rubble has been removed since they were abandoned. It is likely that during their occupation most of the structures had only four or five courses of stone at their base with the upper portion of the walls and the roof composed of clay and timber. In the Southwest, this kind of clay and wood construction is often referred to as jacal. Somewhat different from the usual rooms in these units are rooms 50 and 51, which are distinctly rectangular and contain unique inventories of artifacts.

The southern unit is quite different from all of the others. It is composed of 12 rectangular and subrectangular rooms that are joined together by low walls that enclose several courtyards. Unlike the rest of the site where most of the building stone is sandstone, 60 percent of the walls in the southern unit were built with basalt (Hoffman 1985). There is considerable rubble in these rooms due to the double thickness of some walls and to the possibility that the walls were full-height masonry. Another unusual aspect of the southern unit is that this area of the site was utilized before some or all of the rooms were constructed. Excavations have revealed a number of pits and possible hearths below the walls.

The northeastern roomblock appears to be a tightly arranged cluster of seven rectangular rooms that may have been built at the same time. The rooms are relatively large (23 m²), but the accumulation of rubble is small, suggesting that the walls may not have been full-height masonry.

The eastern unit is very poorly understood at this time due to the limited excavation in the area and to the presence of basalt boulders on the surface, which makes it difficult to identify wall alignments on the basis of surface indications alone.

We hoped from the onset that the architectural variety at Shoofly Village would help reveal the composition of the community and the nature of the activities that took place there. Even a preliminary examination revealed a number of characteristics indicating that architectural information might be the key to understanding what went on at Shoofly. First, the layout of rooms and enclosed spaces varied from unit to unit. Second, the raw materials used for wall construction varied across the site. Third, the techniques used to build walls differed from unit to unit. And fourth, the shape and size of individual rooms varied widely across the site and sometimes even within a single unit. I think it is fair to say that at most sites in the Southwest these architectural dimensions are uniform or, at least, exhibit a consistent pattern within an individual community, yet here at Shoofly all four varied widely! This remarkable diversity, we believed, required further investigation and explanation.

In order to explore further the fascinating architectural differences and similarities in the settlement, we planned a second and third stage of excavations.

In Stage II, we dug 14 1 m by 2 m trenches within randomly selected structures from each of the seven architectural groupings or units. This stage of the investigation provided additional information on the artifacts, ecofacts, and features associated with the structures and an initial understanding of the nature of the different building traditions, which was quickly becoming the prime question confronting us.

In Stage III, which we pursued during each subsequent season, we selected 20 areas to be excavated on a judgmental, rather than a random, basis in order to address specific interpretive questions. During Stage III, we expanded Stage II excavations in most of the rooms tested, exploring the rooms further and opening adjacent outdoor areas. For example, room 51 in the northern periphery was first test excavated during Stage II, revealing unusual artifacts (e.g., grooved axes, polishing stones, and many projectile points) and what appeared to be a flagstone floor. During Stage III, excavations in room 51 were expanded from the initial 1 m by 2 m unit to the entire room in order to determine the character of floor features and recover the full range of artifacts that remained there. In the following season, a nearby room, number 50, was also completely excavated.

The excavations during the following three field seasons (1985, 1986, and 1987) continued the three-phase excavation strategy of the original field season, but they were also concerned with gaining additional information on site-wide patterns. It was clear that many activities took place outside the rooms at Shoofly, just as they did at many other sites. This led us to continue our excavations in areas adjacent to, but outside, the sampled rooms. In this way we hoped to uncover evidence of the full range of activities that was associated with the people living in the room.

Moreover, we expected that other kinds of activities had occurred in the large enclosed south plaza and, possibly, outside the enclosure wall. In an effort to recover this information, we placed 20 randomly selected 0.5 m by 2.0 m trenches outside the compound wall and 4 judgmentally selected trenches in the open plaza area in the southern portion of the site (south plaza). During these excavations, we were successful in exposing middens, burials, and hidden features. Middens were encountered both inside and outside the compound wall. Within the compound wall in the south plaza area several outside features, including hearths, shallow pits, a lightly built structure, and associated activity areas, were discovered. The stratigraphic association of at least some of these features with nearby architecture indicated that they predated the construction of the south roomblock.

To explore the variability among architectural groupings further, we conducted additional excavations of rooms originally tested in Stage II and others identified from the surface map during each field season. The initial Stage II trench was usually expanded to approximately one-fourth of the room and, if the discoveries merited further work, the entire room was excavated. The information recovered from the rooms in the initial Stage II sampling design often led us to investigate other nearby or similarly shaped rooms as part of Stage III. In most rooms at Shoofly it was very difficult to identify floors because they were not carefully made. Thus, it required considerable time to recognize and expose floor features. During the final 1987 field season, considerable effort was expended to carefully examine floor and subfloor areas in rooms already excavated. Taken altogether, the total excavation sample at Shoofly reached 20 rooms, 50 extramural units inside the compound, and 20 soundings outside the compound wall.

Prehistoric Growth of Shoofly Village

In order to understand the nature of the community at Shoofly Village more clearly, it is useful to review the evidence in a manner that reflects the growth of the settlement. Unlike many other large Southwestern sites, Shoofly was not built in a single episode but rather grew over a long period of time. In fact, the successive incorporation of what appear to have been independent social groups into the community and the continuation of some signs of their autonomy are distinguishing characteristics of the settlement and demand our closest examination. Consequently, I propose a four-phase sequence for the growth of Shoofly Village and present the evidence by phase (Fig. 5.7). This framework is a revision of earlier work by Laurene Montero (1989), and I expect that as research proceeds it will be revised once again. Despite its tentative nature, I strongly believe that a trial formulation such as this chronology allows the scholar and lay reader alike to gain a better perspective on the evidence.

The first phase at Shoofly Village may have started with the construction of several free-standing curved-wall structures, such as rooms 35, 41, and 52. It may also have begun with the building of a somewhat more integrated group of three or four rooms, such as the complex that comprises rooms 31, 32, and 33. In any case, phase 1 would include most of the structures located in the western, northwestern, northern, and eastern units. I expect that new rooms or groups of rooms were added slowly, indicating a relatively long duration for phase 1.

The geographic location of early Shoofly proved favorable over time, and as many as 20 or 25 individual and grouped structures were built in a roughly semicircular layout with an opening toward the south. In the south was a flat area that may been the site of

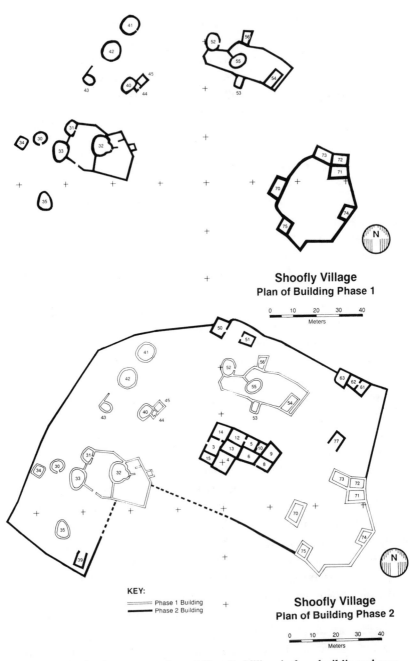

Shoofly Village
Plan of Building Phase 1

0   10   20   30   40
Meters

KEY:
===== Phase 1 Building
——— Phase 2 Building

Shoofly Village
Plan of Building Phase 2

0   10   20   30   40
Meters

5.7   Hypothesized reconstruction of Shoofly Village's four building phases.

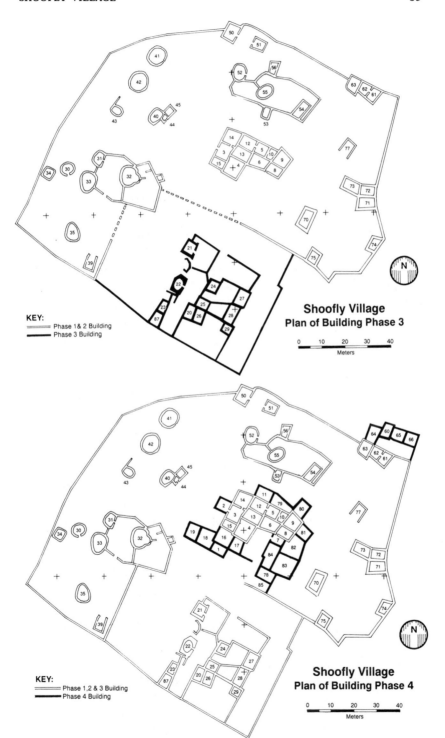

KEY:
Phase 1 & 2 Building
Phase 3 Building

Shoofly Village
Plan of Building Phase 3

0   10   20   30   40
Meters

KEY:
Phase 1,2 & 3 Building
Phase 4 Building

Shoofly Village
Plan of Building Phase 4

0   10   20   30   40
Meters

communal activities, as evidenced by the presence of hearths, ramadas, trash disposal, and burials. It is not known how many of the low walls that separated some areas and connected others were built during this first phase. My guess is that as more individual structures were built at Shoofly, residents began to partition their space and officially separate from others. The flat, open area toward the south would have been used by everyone and thus would have a special importance to the entire community.

On the basis of a few early radiocarbon dates and a scattering of early diagnostic ceramics, I would date phase 1 to about A.D. 900–1050, or the second half of Wood's Union Park phase. The structures assigned to phase 1 were probably built in several distinct episodes spanning this considerable period of time. The early settlers of Shoofly seem to have built at least some houses-in-pits, but they did not use Hohokam ceramics, in contrast with some of their neighbors a few kilometers to the southwest. In fact, the absence of Hohokam ceramics is surprising and may reflect a deliberate effort by the early occupants of Shoofly to separate themselves from Hohokam influence.

The second phase of growth at Shoofly encompasses the first construction stages of the core roomblock and the enclosure wall. During this phase all rooms were constructed in a rectangular shape and the preferred building material was sandstone, although some basalt and limestone were also used. I would suggest that about half of the core roomblock was built at this time, forming a massive L-shaped structure (rooms 3–6, 8–10, and 12–15). Also during this phase several rectangular rooms around the periphery were constructed (rooms 50–51 and 61–63). A large part of the enclosure wall was also built, enclosing all of the village's structures.

The building of the core roomblock and compound wall signal a transformation in the nature of the community at Shoofly Village and may have required a substantial period of time to accomplish. Up to this point, the groups that lived at Shoofly mirrored the small-scale household communities or small hamlets that already characterized the Payson-Star Valley area. Moreover, the phase 1 construction techniques tended toward lightly built structures with little evidence of a planned layout to the settlement. The core roomblock, however, represents a departure from these traditions. Construction of its massive walls and contiguous rooms required close cooperation, if not actual-controlled planning. The placement of the core roomblock on the large flat area that had previously been used for communal activities may signify the elevated position its residents assumed within the community. Additional evidence that the people of the core roomblock may have wielded extra influence is the enclosure of the entire settlement by the building of the compound wall. Although this wall was not particularly high, it clearly delineated the site and all those who lived within it. The many person-days required for its construction implies a high level of cooperative effort, if not outright control. It is not possible to know the duration of phase 2 with certainty, but the extent of its construction indicates a relatively long time, perhaps lasting from A.D. 1050–1150, the beginning of the chronological Payson phase.

Once again Shoofly Village had retained its roughly semicircular layout, with a plaza area to the south. The new arrivals built their dwellings on what was previously communal land. Phase 3 involved the construction of the south roomblock and the extension of the compound wall around it. The combination of individual rooms linked by short walls that enclosed courtyards is reminiscent of Shoofly's earlier phase 1 compounds, but the layout is denser and more rectangular, and the construction is somewhat more massive.

Whether the south roomblock or the compound wall around it came first is difficult to discern, but our guess is that they were built together and not long after the core roomblock was completed. Without implying too much precision, I would suggest that this episode fell toward the middle of Wood's chronological Payson phase, about A.D. 1150–1200.

Phase 4 was a period of filling-in of the site: that is, a doubling of the size of the core roomblock, the addition of rooms outside what was then the enclosure wall (rooms 60 and 64–66), as well as the continued utilization of rooms around the entire site. As in phase 3, the alterations of phase 4 may have occurred rapidly, perhaps in as little time as a generation. The additions to the core roomblock doubled its size but, although the floor area of some of the rooms was quite large, the masonry in their walls may not have been full height. I would suggest that phase 4 rooms may have been built by new immigrants, closely associated with the people who lived in the core roomblock, but coming from a tradition of lightly constructed architecture, like the peripheral groups that first settled Shoofly Village in phase 1.

The depositional evidence from various excavations indicates that phase 4 may have had a relatively short duration, dating to A.D. 1200–1250 or slightly later. It is important to emphasize that virtually all areas of the site appear to have remained in use until very near the end of Shoofly's occupation. Of course, there were probably one or two rooms in each part of the village that did go out of use; during our excavations, we found a few rooms that contained the kind of post-occupational trash deposition that one would expect from an abandoned room (room 41 had dense trash and room 25 had a burial in the fill). Nevertheless, Shoofly Village in A.D. 1200–1225 probably looked very much like the complete map we have made. The fact that what appears to have been distinct groups remained together in a small community is very much at the heart of the Shoofly story.

BUILDING PHASE I

The majority of structures built during phase 1 have subrectangular or curved-wall shapes. Some are free standing and built into shallow pits (about 30 cm deep), while others are founded at ground level and have low wing walls attached to them. From the surface a few ground-level rooms appeared to be rectangular, but after excavation all of the tested examples were found to have rounded corners. Hence, I believe we may assume that this is true of the currently unexcavated rooms as well. The phase 1 structures are preserved at most a few stones high and on the average contain shallow (less than 0.5 m) deposits. This reflects a simple depositional history of a floor zone with one or more remodellings and a post-occupational fill deposit. It should be noted that the density of artifacts in phase 1 buildings is the highest on the site (averaging over 1,000 pieces per cubic meter). One explanation for this may be that some of the structures were abandoned before others in the settlement and, consequently, became trash dumps for the rest of the community. A second possibility is that, due to the low walls and thin post-occupational deposit, the artifacts left there were condensed into a smaller volume of dirt, yielding higher density figures. What is interesting is that the density of artifacts found in the floor zone is also higher for these buildings, a fact that has not been explained.

5.8   View of room 52 in building phase 1 at Shoofly Village. Entryway is in the foreground and depressions are hearths and in-floor storage pits.

Another significant aspect of phase 1 structures is that their plan, size, and contents are quite different from one another. We have excavated all or a major portion of six rooms and the diversity is remarkable. Room 52 is a curvilinear building that was originally built with the floor about 30 cm below ground surface (Fig. 5.8). It was quite large, enclosing almost 30 m², although its masonry foundation was only one or two stones high. It must have been mostly a mud-and-wood structure (jacal). Its floor has revealed traces of internal post supports and two sequentially used hearths near the doorway. The hearths are clay-lined and hemispherical in shape, and the two together indicate a moderately long occupation or reoccupation of the building.

Room 31 is a D-shaped room that is part of a complex of several rooms and enclosed spaces. One of the first impressions we had of this complex was its similarity to a small hamlet, such as the Mud Springs Site (see Chapter 6). Two other rooms (32 and 33), a possible storeroom (room 38), and two unroofed enclosures make up the remainder of the complex. Room 31 was average in size for Shoofly, about 20 m², and its walls were carefully prepared but only two or three stones high. We assume that the remainder of the walls were made of jacal. A variety of small postholes, pits, and a single clay-lined hearth were found in the floor.

Room 41 is a substantially larger subrectangular room that was completely rebuilt at least once during its lifetime (Fig. 5.9). It is more than 30 m² in size. Its jacal superstructure was supported by a series of posts around the inside of the low masonry walls and by two posts in the center of the room. It had two distinct floor levels that probably correlate with the two different patterns of postholes. Of equal importance was its abundant artifact inventory. Two very large complete metates were found in the room, one turned upside down adjacent to the entryway, and a second built into a niche in the wall along the southwest side. This second metate was unusual because it had just the beginning of a depression, suggesting either that it had been used for a short period of time or that it was still in the process of being manufactured. A large groundstone and chipped stone assemblage was recovered from room 41, indicating that the room was used for activities related to food preparation and stone tool manufacture. Although room 41 yielded more artifacts than any other room at Shoofly, it failed to produce any ornamental stone pieces or polishing stones, both related to ceremonial activities and personal adornment.

BUILDING PHASE 2

The phase 2 buildings exhibit a new construction technique that may reflect changes in the composition of the people involved in building them and, perhaps, a change in the authority structure of the community. During this phase rectangular rooms were constructed, most notably an array of contiguous rooms to the south of the existing phase 1 structures at what ultimately became the center of the settlement. A few rectangular rooms scattered around the periphery, or at least on the northern margin, were also built. We expect that it was during this period that most of the enclosure wall was built. The construction of the various roomblocks and enclosure wall may have occurred independently of each other and over a period of time. Most importantly, however, the phase 2 portion of what became the core roomblock appears to have been built as a unit, which would have required plan-

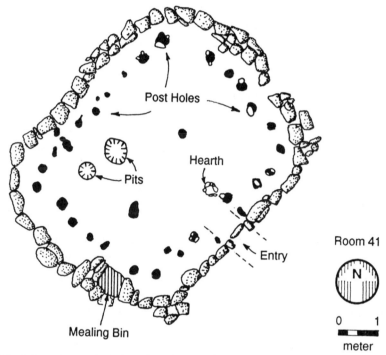

5.9   Map of room 41 in building phase 1, Shoofly Village.

ning and cooperation among group members. Although it is speculative, we believe that the movement of a more organized group into the
core roomblock was associated with the building of some specialized
outlying rooms, such as 50 and 51.

The rooms in what eventually became the core roomblock are made
of double-laid, full-height masonry walls. We suggest that the initial
phase 2 construction included at least six rooms (4–6, 10, 12–13) and
maybe as many as twelve. The core rooms vary in size, but on the
average they are the largest at Shoofly, often extending over 30 m² in
area. Of the phase 2 core roomblock rooms, we excavated number 5
completely and tested numbers 4 and 6. Room 5 appears to have been
built later than the rooms to the south and west, although this may have
been part of a single building episode with very little time passing
between the construction of room 5 and its neighbors. There is evidence

for earlier living surface features below what we identified as the floor associated with room 5. The pits, postholes, and hearth may reflect activities that took place at this location during phase 1, or they may indicate that this area was used as an outside space by residents of the adjacent and somewhat earlier core rooms to the south or west during phase 2.

Room 5 was smaller than average for the roomblock, being only 22 m² in area, yet it contained our best-preserved series of ceramic vessels (Fig. 5.10). At least 13 pots were recovered in largely complete, though crushed, condition. They were found in the roof fall, which might indicate that at least some of them were suspended from the ceiling, actually resting on top of the roof for use in a second story, or outside on the roof. Almost all of the reconstructible vessels were large jars, two of which had volumes of 14 and 41 liters (Montero 1989). The rest of the artifact inventory consisted of expected quantities of lithic material and food residues. Of interest, though, was a smaller than expected number of groundstone pieces, and more than the average number of worked argillite and turquoise stone fragments. The presence of a relatively large hearth (0.5 m in diameter) that had been relined several times suggests that at least some food preparation activities took place there. Taken together, this evidence seems to indicate that, although the normal range of domestic activities occurred within this room, those who used it were involved more with the storage of plant materials than with their processing. In addition, they spent some of their time in the manufacture of ornamental stone artifacts.

Although it is difficult to correlate the construction of widely separated rooms at Shoofly, I am postulating that several outlying rectangular rooms, including numbers 50 and 51, were constructed during this phase. These two rooms are lined up almost next to each other along the northern edge of the site and abut the enclosure wall. They are both moderately large, of doubled-laid, primarily sandstone construction. Their size and technology parallel that of the core rooms, except that they did not appear to have had full-height stone walls. Both rooms had hearths and their doorways faced each other across what appears to be a passageway, possibly leading to outside the site. Room 50 had a normal range of artifacts, with a relatively high proportion of lithics and projectile points.

5.10   Ceramic vessels crushed in place found in room 5 of building phase 2, Shoofly Village.

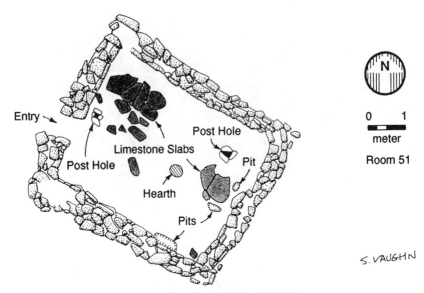

5.11   Map of room 51 in building phase 2, Shoofly Village.

Room 51 had one of the most distinctive assemblages of the entire
site, as well as the only occurrence of several limestone slabs that appear
to have served as partial flooring (Fig. 5.11). Noteworthy in the lithic
assemblage from room 51 were polishing stones, tabular knives, and 14
projectile points. In addition, there were quartz crystals, stalactites,
malachite pieces, slate ornaments, and worked argillite. Also unusual
for Shoofly was the room's groundstone inventory, with over twenty
manos, as well as rubbing stones, anvils, and four polished axes or
mauls. The ceramics from both rooms were not unusually abundant or
diverse. The overall impression is of the manufacture and varied use of
stone materials for tools, ornaments, and food preparation. This evidence and the location of the rooms near the site perimeter suggest that
they were used for specialized activities, perhaps associated with off-site
activities to the north.

BUILDING PHASE 3

The growth of Shoofly Village continued with the construction of a
roomblock to the south of the newly established core roomblock. This

dispersed grouping is made up of about twelve rooms and five enclosed spaces. The layout of the rooms, with one or two rooms associated with an adjacent unroofed, enclosed space, suggests that they housed small family or task units that functioned more or less independently. Stratigraphic evidence indicates that this area had contained outdoor features, such as ramadas and hearths, before the roomblock was built. Although the surface indications of the south roomblock suggest rectangular architecture, the two rooms (21 and 22) we excavated have rounded corners and double-thick front walls. Other than one large room, which may actually be an enclosed outdoor space, the south roomblock has modest-sized rooms, averaging 20 m². Unlike all of the other roomblocks, this one is built primarily of basalt boulders. I believe that at about this same time the final portion of the compound wall was constructed to enclose all of the various structures and roomblocks. It is noteworthy that this part of the compound wall is also composed primarily of basalt boulders.

Room 21, which was completely excavated, revealed at least two occupation episodes within the room and possibly an earlier occupation on that spot before the room was built (Fig. 5.12). A small stone-lined hearth was built inside the doorway and small pits were dug into both floor levels. One of the pits, however, was quite large and may have been used for roasting items too large for the hearth. Moreover, a series of postholes were found around the pit suggesting that a wooden scaffold might have been used to elevate meat or hides above the pit. The room contained a relatively ordinary ceramic and lithic inventory and an abundant groundstone assemblage. One item of special interest was a piece of sandstone bedrock that protruded through the floor and had five small circular depressions or cupules (Fig. 5.13). This may have been used for grinding pigments or other fine materials. Also in the room was a long, thin double-ended pestle that may have been used in conjunction with the bedrock mortar. It may also have had some ceremonial significance since its form is similar to pieces called wands at other sites.

The construction of the enclosure, or compound wall, surrounding the various architectural units at Shoofly Village required a tremendous amount of effort. It was about 550 m in length and, in the few places we cross-sectioned it, the wall was 0.7 m or more across and about 1.0 m

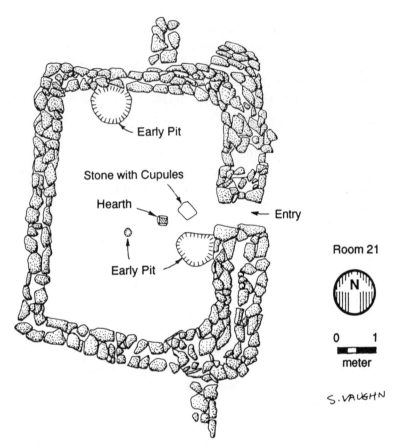

5.12   Map of room 21 in building phase 3, Shoofly Village.

high. Its dimensions suggest that at least 400 m³ of stones had to be moved and piled to form the wall. Although it was probably constructed in segments over a period of years, it still represents a major effort on the part of the people of Shoofly and something they would not do without a reason. There are two hypotheses for why the wall would have been built. The first is that it was built as an immediate effort to defend the community because of conflict in the region. Shoofly's location in an open setting on top of Houston Mesa and toward the northern end of settlement in the region lends support to the defense hypothesis. If it were true, we would expect the stone wall to have been

5.13   View of room 21, Shoofly Village. Note the stone-lined hearth, boulder with cupules, and oblong pestle on the floor. Entryway is in the foreground and dark areas to the left are in-floor storage pits.

surmounted by a lighter and higher type of construction, such as logs, mud, or branches. We have no evidence of that nor of any active warfare, which would be indicated by trauma wounds on skeletal material or by caches of weapons. Nevertheless, it may have been built for defense, whether or not it was actively needed.

An alternative hypothesis, which is harder to back with evidence, relates to the human tendency to physically mark off social space and boundaries. From this perspective, the various isolated walls within the community would have demarcated social divisions within the community and the massive compound wall would have symbolically and physically enclosed the entire settlement as a unit. Although it does not have the urgency of the first hypothesis, I favor this explanation because I regard the construction of the core roomblock as a transformation of what had been a loose assembly of rural family groups from different backgrounds into a unified settlement, perhaps with a dominant group at the geographic center. In this way Shoofly Village can be seen as something of a prehistoric "melting pot."

BUILDING PHASE 4

During the final phase of construction at Shoofly Village, a new room-block was built in the northeast corner of the site and rooms were added to the core roomblock. They were built primarily of sandstone and in a rectangular pattern with double-laid walls. The structures, including the additional rooms around the core roomblock, may not have had full height masonry walls. At the same time that this final burst of building activity occurred, I suspect that some phase 1 and, possibly, phase 2 structures were abandoned. I also expect that in both phases 3 and 4, the use of outdoor space became more constrained due to the filling-in of the settlement. Such outdoor activities as hide and food preparation probably continued in the enclosed spaces adjacent to the rooms. Other activities, such as trash dumping and burial, were probably moved to the exterior of the compound wall, possibly to the southeast or north or in newly abandoned rooms like 41.

Most of the new core roomblock rooms built during phase 4 are poorly known. Only one of them was investigated by more than a small test excavation unit. Room 7 appears to have been added to the south-east corner of the existing core in an area that was previously used for pits (Fig. 5.14). Room 7 was relatively small for the core roomblock, enclosing only 17.5 m². It was built at one end of a new wing of rooms that transformed the shape of the block from an L to a U. The area had been used for at least two episodes of outdoor activity before the con-struction of the room. The earliest use is reflected in a deposit of scattered trash that may have resulted from more distant activities during phase 1. Above that was an ash-filled pit that ran under the west wall and probably was used by people from nearby core rooms during phase 2 or 3.

The floor surface associated with room 7 itself may have had more than one episode of use. Three small hearths were found within the room and floor-type features and deposits had accumulated to a depth of almost 30 cm. The most distinctive artifact in these deposits was a very large and very worn trough metate that could be associated with the final use of the room (Fig. 5.15). Two niches were built into the north wall of room 7, one of them defined by a limestone slab lintel. The artifact inventory included some ornamental objects, but not an

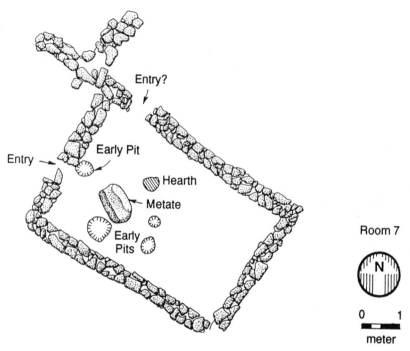

Entry?

Entry

Early Pit

Hearth

Metate

Early Pits

Room 7

N

0   1
meter

5.14   Map of room 7 in building phase 4, Shoofly Village.

unusual quantity. Overall, the artifacts reflected the range of domestic activities characteristic of Shoofly.

From surface indications, most of the other additions to the core roomblock appear to be unusually large rooms that probably did not have full-height masonry walls. This opens the possibility that some of the "rooms" may, in fact, be unroofed enclosed outdoor spaces adjacent to the normal core rooms. It is also possible that toward the end of Shoofly's occupation less effort was devoted to construction, with stone used only for the foundations and jacal for the superstructures. Whether or not the construction quality remained the same, phase 4 witnessed the growth of, and the concentration of people in, the core roomblock to a point where it quite clearly dominated the site.

5.15   View of room 7 with large, well-worn metate, Shoofly Village.

The north roomblock also remains enigmatic in our understanding of the site. This tightly packed roomblock is located at an extreme corner of the site at the highest elevation, thereby commanding a view of the rest of the settlement. We have excavated portions of three rooms in the block. They range from large to average size and all are rectangular and contiguous. My own belief is that room 63, and possibly others, were actually built before the compound wall was erected during phase 2 or 3, and then, during phase 4, additional rooms were built as part of the filling in of the site. The artifacts have not distinguished this part of the site as specializing in one activity or another. The only special architectural information comes from room 60 where the walls seem to consist of two sets of concentric walls separated by about 30 cm of space. It is not clear what purpose that would have served except, perhaps, to form the foundation of a platform or raised floor. The relatively low number of artifacts found in phase 4 rooms is expected since there were no later occupants in the village to dump trash in their rooms. The low walls and lack of rubble fill is more surprising and may reflect a diminished ability to marshall the labor and resources that must have been required to build the substantial architecture of the original core rooms.

ABANDONMENT

We have little information concerning the abandonment of Shoofly Village, but the stratigraphic evidence indicates that most of the rooms were occupied right up until the end. This is based on the relative absence of trash deposits above the roof and wall fall in most rooms. If this conclusion is true, then very near its peak occupation the settlement was abandoned and the inhabitants moved elsewhere. Several central rooms in the core roomblock show clear evidence of burning, which may have been one of the factors leading to abandonment. However, prehistoric settlements often burned down for a variety of reasons, but the people usually overcame the hardship and rebuilt their homes.

Another line of evidence comes from the ceramics. If the ceramic chronology is correct, then some of the other villages in the creek zone to the south continued to be occupied somewhat later than Shoofly. Our best estimate is that Shoofly was largely abandoned by A.D. 1225 or 1250. By contrast, surface sherds indicate that Risser Ranch in Payson and Mayfield Canyon in Star Valley (as well as Round Valley further south) may have been occupied a generation or two longer, until the end of the thirteenth century. This could indicate that settlement contracted into the creek zone or that the focus of activity and settlement in the region moved toward the south. I suspect that it was some of both and will return to this subject in Chapter 10.

6 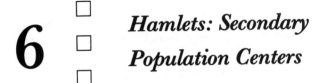 *Hamlets: Secondary Population Centers*

Interspersed among the primary villages of the Payson-Star Valley region are intermediate-sized settlements, with from six to as many as forty rooms (Fig. 6.1). These hamlets reflect communities of various population sizes, ranging from a few families to more than 100 people. In our study area we have investigated eight of these sites (see Figure 4.2) and the Tonto National Forest records document approximately twice this number. Although more numerous than primary villages, these numbers are not large, indicating a proportion of only one or two hamlets for each primary village. The question of whether hamlets are associated with individual villages in a dependent manner is not simple to answer, but it is crucial to an understanding of the overall settlement system.

A study based on ceramic petrography—the microscopic identification of the mineral constituents of a piece of ceramic—implies that strong ties may have existed between specific hamlets and villages. A compositional analysis of plainware ceramics conducted by Burton (1988) and Simon (1988) indicates that a significant proportion of the ceramics found at a hamlet called Site 620—and at other hamlets as well—could only have been produced on Houston Mesa, and probably

6.1   Artist's reconstruction of the small hamlet, Mud Springs. (By Jon Joha.)

at Shoofly Village, a primary village. More recent work by Burton and Simon indicates that a similar relationship existed between the village of Risser Ranch and a hamlet near it, Deer Jaw Ruin. We expect that with further analyses other site pairings, which reflect regular interaction and exchange of goods, will be discovered. Interestingly, the many potsherds examined from Shoofly Village reveal an unusual degree of compositional homogeneity, indicating that the inhabitants produced almost all of their own pottery. Hence, Shoofly Village did not depend on the surrounding hamlets for a supply of pottery, but rather supplied them with a substantial proportion of their ceramic inventory. It has been suggested that the relationship between villages and hamlets might have taken the form of an actual movement of part or all of the people in the hamlet to one of the villages for part of the year (Hohmann 1988a). This movement might have been related to a ceremonial cycle that brought people together from various communities. Gathering in the village for ceremonies would also have provided the people with an opportunity to exchange goods and information and to establish marriage partnerships. At this point in our analysis, however, we have only documented the movement of ceramics from a primary village to a secondary hamlet in two cases, and we have no archaeological evidence to confirm or refute the hypothesis that hamlet dwellers moved seasonally to one of the larger village settlements.

The choice of a site for a hamlet seems to be related as much to appropriate topography and available resources as it is to proximity to a primary village. Around the village of Risser Ranch, the closest-known hamlet, Deer Jaw Ruin, is less than half a kilometer to the east and other hamlets, such as Pinyon Ruin and 04-144, are within 1.5 km. The situation around Shoofly Village is quite different. The closest-known hamlets are 04-59, which is 2 km to the south; 04-35, 3 km to the east; and Sunflower Mesa Ruin, more than 4 km to the northwest. We may be witnessing two distinct settlement patterns. One is that of the Payson Basin where Risser Ranch and other sites are unevenly spaced to take advantage of the high ridges surrounding the agricultural lowlands. This contrasts sharply with the settlement pattern in the open high country of the Houston Mesa area where Shoofly Village and the surrounding hamlets are more evenly spaced at 2 to 4 km intervals.

Deer Jaw Ruin

Deer Jaw Ruin, whose name derives from an abundance of deer mandibles found in one of its rooms, occupies the top of a high hill with vistas in three directions (Hohmann and Atwell 1988). It is only a short distance east of an even higher hill where Risser Ranch Ruin, the largest prehistoric settlement in the Payson area, is located. Because of their close proximity, we assume that the two communities interacted regularly, perhaps providing support services for each other. A preliminary petrographic analysis of the ceramics found at the two sites supports the hypothesis of close interaction; the pottery at both sites was evidently manufactured in one place, probably at Risser Ranch (Simon 1988).

Although people may have moved in and out of the Deer Jaw Ruin settlement, we have found material evidence of a full range of domestic activities, which indicates that the site was occupied throughout the year. Individual rooms are large, and they yielded a diversity of features and artifacts. From differences in the construction of various

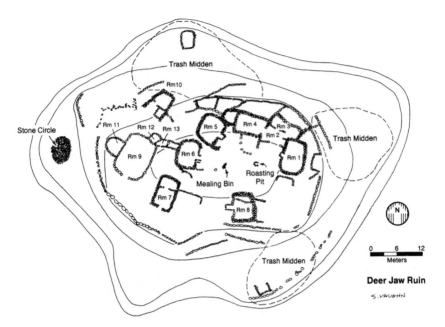

6.2   Overall map of Deer Jaw Ruin.

rooms and in the arrangement of walls, Hohmann and Atwell
(1988:150) have identified what may be three building episodes in the
life of Deer Jaw Ruin.

Although differences in building methods may be most easily
explained as a succession of building periods, I will review the architecture at the site in terms of different construction styles without attempting
to associate each style with a time period. As at Shoofly Village, the
construction methods may represent an architectural style used by different social groups, the evolution of a single building tradition over time,
or a functional customization to accommodate different needs within a
single community. Possibly all of these factors were at work at Deer Jaw
Ruin, as well as at many other sites in the Payson region. Just as I have
argued that over time Shoofly Village may have grown to include small
groups from diverse cultural backgrounds, I suggest that a clustering of
different groups also may have occurred at some of the hamlets.

Large subrectangular rooms formed what perhaps was the primary
occupation unit at Deer Jaw Ruin (rooms 1, 5, 6, and 8 on Figure 6.2).

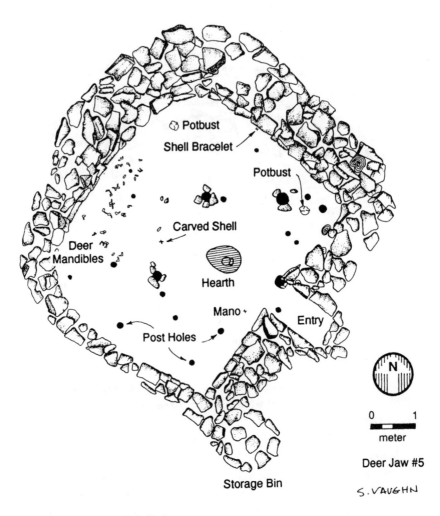

6.3   Room 5, Deer Jaw Ruin.

The rooms are more than 20 m² in area and have traces of postholes, confirming that they were roofed. They also contain a rich variety of features and artifacts reflecting the wide range of activities that occurred in them. Especially noteworthy is room 5, from which over 55 deer mandibles were recovered (Fig. 6.3). Other than this unprecedented concentration of jaw bones, the room was quite ordinary with an entrance to the east, a hearth near the entrance, and two central post supports. A substantial quantity of other animal remains were also found in this room, lending support to the idea that hunting was a primary activity of the room's occupants; ceremonial use may or may not explain the abundance of deer jaws.

The three other subrectangular rooms (1, 6, and 8) are all large, ranging from 20 m² to 33 m² in area. They all have hearths, postholes, and artifacts that reflect their primary function as a living space. The smallest of the group, Room 8, which is situated at one end of the site, had an unusual stone and clay bench across its northern end and a ramada built against the outside of its eastern wall. All four rooms are situated in such a way that they border what may have served as a shared courtyard for outdoor activities. In this area we have uncovered a mealing bin and a roasting pit, and we expect that other features were present.

Rooms 2, 3, and 4 are less well defined. They appear to have been built to fill in the space between structures constructed earlier and to serve as habitation rooms but are not built with the regularity of the original rooms. Rooms 12 through 17 are all quite small and probably served as storage facilities.

Rooms 7 and 10 both have more angular corners, interior partition walls, and entrances that pass through a lightly built south wall. At least in the case of room 7, its size, floor features, and artifacts indicate that it was used for work activities, if not for a full range of habitation activities (Fig. 6.4). Room 10 is less well understood but, because it is devoid of floor features, its primary function might have been storage.

Room 9 represents a much different kind of structure. It is more than 60 m² in area but has lightly built foundation walls (Fig. 6.5). There are some postholes indicating that at least a portion of the room was roofed, but I doubt whether the entire structure was covered. Given that most of the other rooms at Deer Jaw were constructed with thick, high foundation walls, the contrast with room 9 is great. The artifact assemblage from this room is small, but it is distinguished by a relatively high proportion of sherds from imported decorated ceramic vessels (see Hohmann and Atwell 1988:164). Our best hypothesis is that this was a room for ceremonial purposes where some work activities might have been conducted or goods exchanged. The presence of small storage rooms (11–13) abutting room 9 adds support to this interpretation.

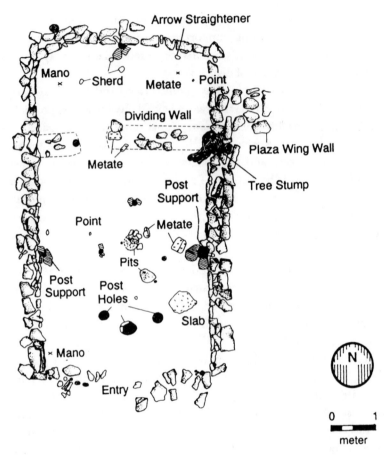

6.4   Room 7, Deer Jaw Ruin.

Pinyon Ruin

The hamlet known as Pinyon Ruin is located on a ridge top overlooking Star Valley along the eastern edge of the hills that separate Payson from Star Valley. Based on the relative scarcity of artifactual and ecofactual

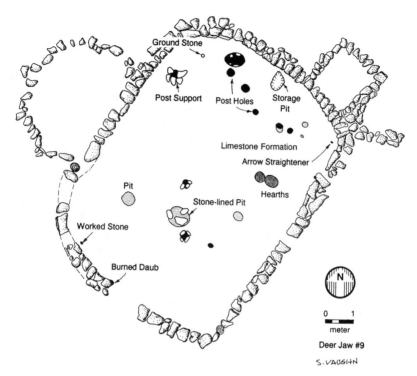

6.5 Room 9, Deer Jaw Ruin.

material, Hohmann and Gregory (1988) suggest that Pinyon Ruin was occupied only intermittently, perhaps on a seasonal basis. One particularly interesting aspect of the settlement is that the layout of its rooms resembles that of Shoofly Village, although on a smaller scale (Fig. 6.6). The most obvious similarity is the dichotomy between a series of rectilinear rooms built into a contiguous roomblock (rooms 3–7) and two separate subrectangular rooms (numbers 1–2). Also like Shoofly, Pinyon Ruin has a well-preserved enclosure wall along its south and east sides and the remains of what might possibly have been an extension of the wall around the remainder of the hamlet.

Although the features and artifacts are not abundant, the existing evidence indicates that all seven rooms were used for habitation. The rooms average about 20 m^2 in area, with the free-standing subrectangular rooms slightly larger than those in the roomblock. The walls of the

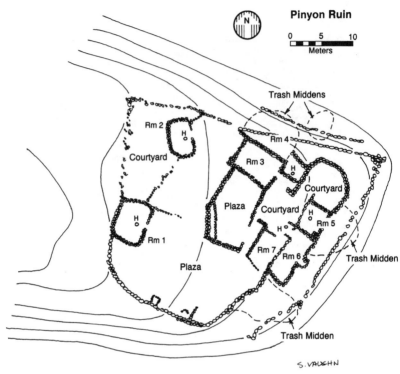

6.6   Overall map of Pinyon Ruin.

rectangular roomblock rooms exhibit more regular construction with
rocks of selected shapes or even shaped stones (Fig. 6.7), while the walls
of the two subrectangular rooms show less fashioning and alignment.
Once again, this parallels the building distinctions found at Shoofly. It
should be noted that the geographic location of Pinyon Ruin is within
the Shoofly-Star Valley sphere of activities, which might explain some
of the similarities. Also, the petrographic study by Burton and Simon
(1991) indicates that some ceramic material found at Pinyon Ruin was
almost certainly made at Shoofly Village.

Site 620

Site 620, which has at least 20 rooms, is the largest of the hamlets we
excavated; it is probable, however, that the rooms represent several

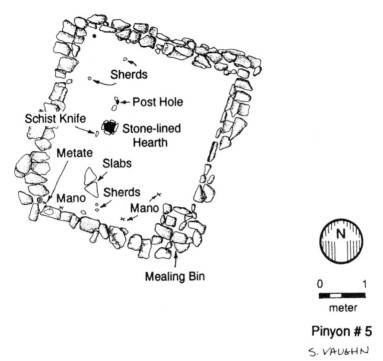

6.7   Room 5, Pinyon Ruin.

consecutive and independent settlements (Bradley 1991b). Site 620 is
located in the creek zone close to the modern town of Star Valley. It is
situated on a low north-south oriented ridge bordered on the east by
Mayfield Canyon drainage and on the west by Houston Creek. Because
of its location, the occupants of the site would have had a reasonably
reliable source of water and considerable arable land close to their
settlement. The proximity of these important resources made this an
extremely favorable location, as the succession of settlements and the
presence of several smaller sites within a short distance demonstrate.
Moreover, about 100 m north of Site 620 on the same ridge is one of the
primary village centers of the region, the Mayfield Canyon site. We
imagine that this entire ridge was occupied continuously between A.D.
1000 and A.D. 1300 by people living in small communities, but that
during the last 100 years the population aggregated into the two larger
settlements, Mayfield Canyon and Site 620.

Because of the narrowness of the ridge, the buildings of Site 620 are physically separated into two groups—a north and a south component (Fig. 6.8). Although the exact relationship between the people who lived in these roomblocks is unknown, it is likely that they interacted frequently with one another and with inhabitants of nearby sites, and that they may have belonged to a larger social group. After Shoofly Village, Site 620 exhibits the greatest amount of architectural diversity in the sites we excavated, probably representing three distinct construction phases. What is important here, as I believe it was at Shoofly, is that the older structures seem to have remained in use, while later construction phases incorporated new building techniques and layout principles. Whether this represents the introduction of new people or new ideas or an evolution in the approach to building by the same people is difficult to know. What is clear, however, is that significant architectural diversity existed within individual settlements, both large and small. This is a surprising archaeological discovery since if this reflects the fact that the inhabitants of these settlements were comprised of diverse groups, it indicates that they had developed the organizational means to hold themselves together in closely knit communities for substantial periods of time. This is considered a landmark achievement in social organization and something we did not expect to find in this region.

The earliest structures in both components of Site 620 appear to be free-standing subrectangular rooms to the north of later constructions (rooms 1-2, 9, and 22). Room 1 is particularly interesting because it has lightly built stone walls and numerous postholes along its periphery. This type of construction is similar to Hohokam and Mogollon construction that dates to about A.D. 1000. The assignment of a relatively early date is further supported by the recovery, from deposits in the room, of a decorated slate palette fragment that is similar to well-dated material from Hohokam sites. Since other sites and structures in the Payson-Star Valley area are known from this time range, it is reasonable to conclude that at least a very small settlement was present on this location by A.D. 1000.

The other free-standing rooms at Site 620 resemble the surface-level architecture of subrectangular shape that we have found at most sites in region and probably date to A.D. 1100 or A.D. 1150. Room 9 in the

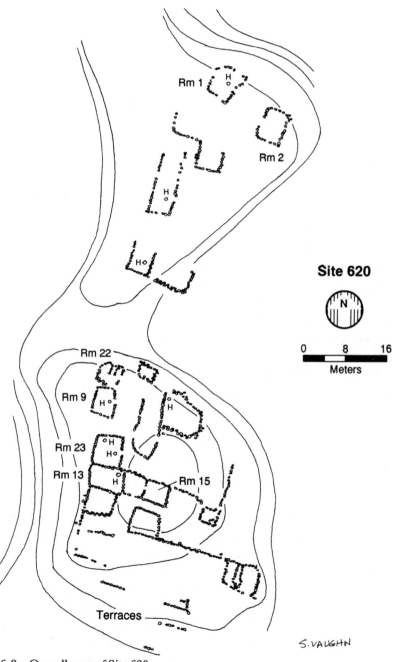

6.8   Overall map of Site 620.

southern component is a nice example of this style. Approximately 20 m² in area, it has lightly built walls consisting of a single row of boulders and a stone-lined hearth in front of the eastern entrance. More information can be deduced from a series of roof beams whose remains were preserved when fire reduced them to carbon. The beams were aligned primarily east to west and spanned the narrower dimension of the room. The pollen found in the early floor deposits consisted primarily of goosefoot, indicating that the area nearby was open country that might have been cleared for farming. By contrast, a majority of pollen grains in subsequent fill deposits came from woody species, particularly juniper, suggesting a period of reforestation during the later occupation of the site. Corn pollen was present in all deposits, reflecting a continued reliance on agriculture throughout its occupation.

The next construction phase at both components of Site 620 resulted in a set of contiguous rectangular rooms laid out in an L-shape or C-shape. The walls of these rooms seemed to be neatly aligned but lightly built. Because of this, the rooms have not retained deep or well-preserved deposits. Each roomblock probably had between eight and ten rooms, representing a moderate-sized community of perhaps 25 to 40 inhabitants.

The final construction phase was either an addition to one of the existing roomblocks or the construction of a new roomblock with the abandonment of the older block of rooms. Between four and six rooms were built in the southern component with carefully selected and sometimes shaped stones arranged in straight, heavily built walls (rooms 13, 15, and 23). The rooms varied in size but averaged over 20 m² in area. Room 23 with almost 26 m² of floor space is one of the largest at the site (Fig. 6.9). The walls were two stones thick with the stones carefully arranged and/or shaped to provide for a smooth wall facing on both the interior and exterior. In addition, a considerable amount of clay mortar was used to solidify the wall. A hearth was located in front of the entrance toward the center of the room. A radiocarbon date from the room had a midpoint of A.D. 1281 (a calibrated one sigma range of A.D. 1260–1388; see Appendix A). The distinctive architectural construction reinforces the late radiocarbon date. It is likely that this roomblock was occupied during the final phase of the major occupation period of the Payson/Star Valley region—the second half of the thirteenth century.

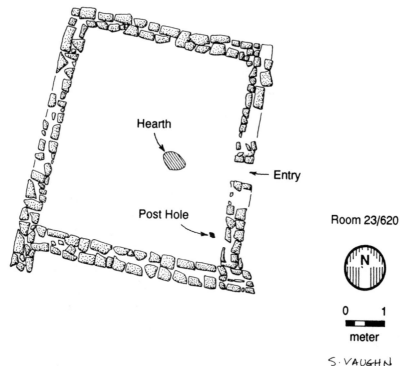

6.9   Room 23, Site 620.

Scorpion Rock Ruin

Scorpion Rock Ruin is another hamlet community overlooking the creek zone near broad arable tracts of land (Hohmann 1988b). The settlement is comprised of an L-shaped roomblock of nine rectangular rooms (Fig. 6.10). Compared with those at other Payson sites, all of the rooms are quite small. Of these, five are large enough to be habitation or work rooms (about 12.5 m² each) and four are so small that they must have been used for storage or specific work tasks (5 m² or less). Of the five larger rooms, the three central units all had hearths and probably were used for the full range of living activities, while the rooms on either end of the roomblock had no hearths and may have been used for a more limited range of activities.

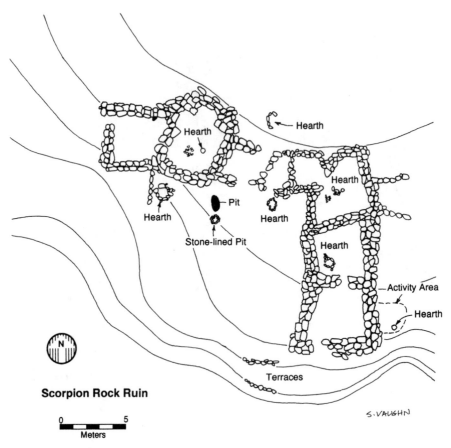

6.10   Overall map of Scorpion Rock Ruin.

The dating of Scorpion Rock Ruin relies mainly on the distinctive ceramics found there. The indications are that it was occupied during the thirteenth century, which is later than most other Payson sites but is similar to the final phase at Site 620. There is, however, a pithouse village located directly below the pueblo construction of Scorpion Rock Ruin that probably dates to A.D. 800–1000. The fact that this location was chosen by one of the earliest groups in the area and also by one of the latest groups indicates the continuing importance of the ridge location that commands a fine view over Green Valley.

Mud Springs Ruin

The Mud Springs Ruin (Fig. 6.11) is a small settlement site that comprised what the excavators interpret as three habitation rooms, four storage rooms, an enclosed plaza, and various work areas (Hohmann and Hohmann 1986). This is very much at the small end of what I would call a hamlet, but the diversity of the components points toward a complex community. The site is located a short distance from Mud Spring, a permanent water source, and is situated on top of a steep knoll that overlooks the confluence of two broad washes that would have provided water for agricultural land. Rooms 1 and 2, along with portions of the compound wall, appear to have been built first. Following that, rooms 3 and 4 were attached to the compound wall with their entrances facing the exterior. Room 1 is interpreted as a habitation room with the adjacent room 2 serving as storage space or, perhaps, for specialized activities. Room 3 is the largest, enclosing about 21 m² of space; a hearth and postholes indicate that it was roofed. Room 4 is also large, enclosing 17 m², but we were unable to find a hearth during excavations. The remaining "rooms" are viewed as storage chambers. Rooms 1, 3, and 4 and a compound wall to the west and north enclose a large space. The features and artifacts found there indicate that it was the locale of outdoor activities and, possibly, the focus of the settlement.

Although construction was constrained by the topography of the steep knoll, the Mud Springs site seems to have been built for a small community of several families. They built subrectangular habitation and storage rooms and felt the need to enclose a large workspace. Some of the room walls were full height while others probably were no more than a meter high, with the remainder built of jacal. Even if we interpret this as a single tightly knit community, it is noteworthy that the construction was accomplished in stages and was not fully coordinated. For example, rooms 3 and 4 are built against the compound wall instead of being utilized as part of the room, and their entrances lead to the exterior instead of to the plaza. Another feature at Mud Springs Ruin that is unusual at small sites is the compound wall, which is normally found only in the larger hamlets and primary village centers of the region. Given these eccentricities, it is especially significant that

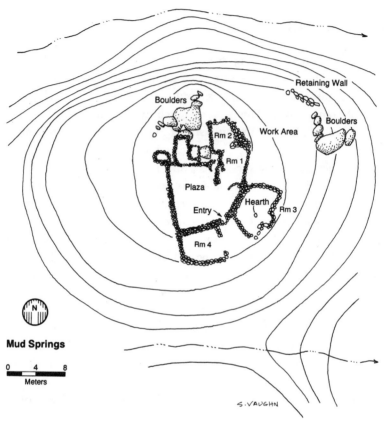

6.11 Overall map of Mud Springs site.

some of the component roomblocks at primary villages in the area exhibit similar features. Specifically, I see a substantial resemblance between the layout of Mud Springs Ruin and the western roomblock established during phase 1 at Shoofly Village. The implication I draw from this is that Mud Springs may have been inhabited by a social unit—an ethnic group or some other distinct group with its own customs—that functioned successfully in both an independent settlement and as a component of a larger community.

Unexcavated Hamlets

During surveys in Tonto National Forest, four additional hamlets that are of particular interest to us were discovered. Three of these are

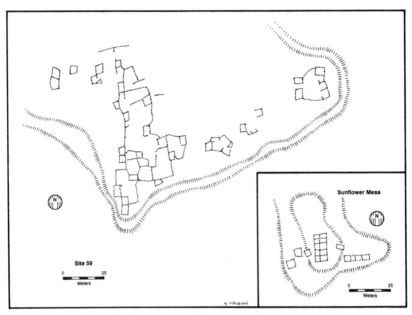

6.12   Sketch maps of other hamlets: Site 59 and Sunflower Mesa.

situated near Shoofly Village, one to the north, one to the south, and one to the southwest (Fig. 6.12). The Sunflower Mesa site (04-23) is situated on top of a small ridge about 4 km north of Shoofly Village. It commands a view of a small valley fed by a seasonal stream that flows directly into the East Verde River. Exact room counts and precise dating are unavailable for the site, but it appears to have contained 15 or more rooms and to overlap in time with Shoofly.

Site 04-59 is located about 2 km south of Shoofly in the broad valley beneath the southern escarpment of Houston Mesa. This site is easily reached from Shoofly, and, since potsherds on the site's surface indicate a similar time range, we assume that its inhabitants were in close contact with the people at Shoofly. It has been very difficult to determine the size or layout of this community since it is in an area of dense vegetation. Surface indications, however, suggest that it included 20 or possibly many more rooms in a dispersed arrangement with compounds of several rooms associated with one or more enclosed spaces. This pattern is similar to that at Pinyon Ruin and in the peripheral areas of Shoofly Village.

In 1991 a new site was recorded about 3 km to the southwest of Shoofly Village. Tentatively named Goat Camp Ruins (04-968), this hamlet contained as many as 30 rooms and was laid out in a long north-south rectangle. Its position along a ridge top commands fine views in all directions.

The fourth site, 04-144, is located at the northern edge of the high ridge that defines the southern extent of the modern town of Payson. It must have been a strategic location in prehistory, overlooking an arable valley and adjacent to a major pass to the south, which is now traversed by State Highway 87. Substantial wall fall indicates that many of its rooms were full-height masonry arranged into one or more roomblocks. We expect that there were at least 20 rooms in the complex and, possibly, twice that number. Although no detailed excavation has been conducted at the site, it would not be surprising to discover that its inhabitants maintained close ties with the people of Risser Ranch village or, perhaps, Round Valley village.

7 □ Household Communities:
□ The Small Sites of the
□ Payson Region

The vast majority of prehistoric sites in the Payson-Star Valley region are quite small, with six or fewer rooms, and some have no surface evidence of architecture at all. These small sites represent the remains of a wide range of activities—from briefly used specialized activity locales to small settlements for one or two families. Within this large and diverse group of sites are many examples of what I believe may be the fundamental settlement type of the Payson region: the household community (see Figure 4.2). For the most part, these appear to have been self-sufficient settlements housing one or two families or a task group defined along other than family lines. Our evidence suggests that the people in these household communities were agriculturalists and that most of their domestic activities took place in these small sites.

Since the areas we surveyed are nonrepresentative because they include only a small portion of the originally settled creek zone, it is difficult to make a reliable estimate of the total number of household communities in the region. Notwithstanding this limitation, it is reasonable to estimate that there were more than 1,000 small sites occupied sometime during A.D. 1000 to A.D. 1300 in the area. In addition to the household communities, about one-fourth of the small sites we investigated in the Payson-Star Valley region consisted of check dams and other agricultural field systems, lightly built hunting and gathering shelters, and artifact scatters with no evidence of built structures. The sites reflect the diversity of activities that accompanied the food gathering pursuits of people who relied on agriculture but who continued to supplement this with wild game hunting and wild plant gathering. Surface indications of sites representing these relatively ephemeral activities are likely to be sparse and, hence, are probably underrepresented among the sites we have discovered. Because this skewing of counts is extremely difficult to correct, it is best to consider the examples we have found as reflecting the range of activities that occurred rather than the actual proportion of any particular activity. One aspect of the picture that emerges from this is that agricultural methods in the Payson-Star Valley were sophisticated to the point where water control was important, especially along the margins of the creek zone. In addition, hunting and collecting stations existed, but not in large numbers, probably reflecting the fact that these activities were supplemental and were integrated into the normal suite of activities taking place at base settlements.

Household Communities

The remainder of this chapter focuses on the small sites that contained architecture and constituted the most basic unit of the Payson settlement system: the household community. If one looks closely at the small sites in the Payson region, one finds that almost every one is unique in some manner. Despite this diversity, it is possible to perceive some general patterns, and it is these similarities that I will emphasize.

The most common structure found on small sites is the free-standing subrectangular room. Site 630 (Fig. 7.1) is centered around a large room of this design, which was built with heavy, rubble core walls (Lindauer 1991d). It is located on a low ridge well away from the creek zone but in an area with washes that might have provided arable land. The main room (number 2) is large with over 24 m² of floor area and with a hearth directly in front of the doorway. While the number of artifacts recovered was relatively low, the substantial nature of the

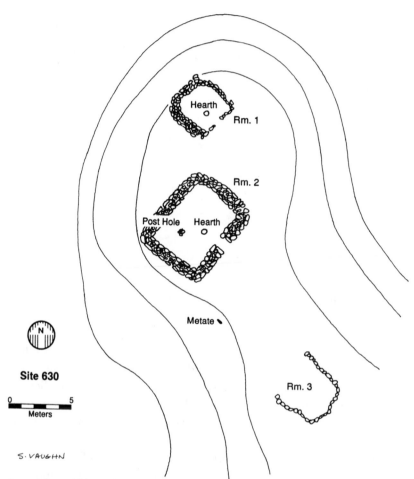

7.1   Map of Site 630.

construction and the large floor area of the room indicate sustained occupation.

In addition to the large room, two other structures were found at Site 630. Both were three-sided structures that we believe were sequentially occupied. Room 1, which was the more heavily built of the two, was similar in construction to the main room. It also had a hearth and may have served as a regular occupation room with a more lightly built fourth wall. Room 3 was very lightly built, defined by only a single row

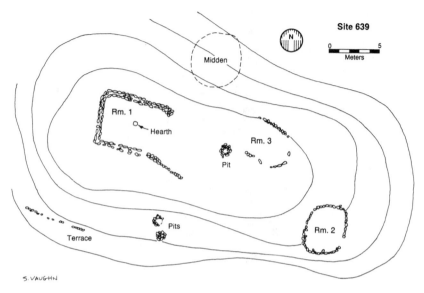

7.2   Map of Site 639.

of stones along its three sides and with no evidence of a hearth or other
floor features. The function of three-sided structures is somewhat enigmatic, but they are present at many sites, ranging from the smallest to
the largest, including Shoofly Village. I expect that in most cases they
were not habitation rooms but served a specialized function for storage
and/or work activities.

More evidence for the use of three-sided rooms comes from Site 639
(Fig. 7.2), located on top of a high ridge south of Star Valley (Lindauer
1991e). Here, in distinction from most sites, the largest and best built
room of the site has only three sides (Fig. 7.3). This room (number 1)
has over 28 m² of floor space and no conclusive evidence for a closure
along the fourth side. The room opens to the southeast and has a wide
range of domestic features, including a hearth and a variety of tools.
The most distinctive remains in the room were from six to twelve
vessels discovered as they had been left. Four vessels were reconstructible, and it was determined, from a profile analysis of the others, that at
most only two of the vessels were bowls and the remainder were jars.
This suggests that a majority of the vessels were used for storage, a

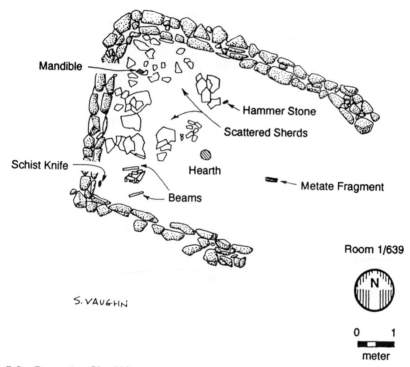

Mandible

Hammer Stone

Scattered Sherds

Schist Knife

Hearth

Metate Fragment

Beams

Room 1/639

S. VAUGHN

N

0   1
meter

7.3   Room 1 at Site 639.

conclusion that is in line with the ceramic inventory of the region in general. It is noteworthy that bowls were present at all since they would be expected to be taken away from a site that was only briefly occupied. Along with a hearth, a metate fragment, a hammerstone, and a schist knife, this material indicated a full range of domestic activities in the room. This is corroborated by the faunal and floral analyses that revealed the remains of diverse foodstuffs, including corn, wild plant material, and at least some large game.

Two other structures, both lightly built, were found at Site 639. Room 3 was also a three-sided room and probably was occupied at the same time as room 1 because they are situated facing each other, enclosing a recognizable work area. Room 2 was an oval structure with a door facing the southeast away from the other two rooms (Fig. 7.4). This room may date to an earlier occupation of the ridge top. Three stone-lined pits were found outside rooms 1 and 3. These appear to have been

7.4   View of lightly built, subrectangular room (room 2), Site 639.

used for both food storage and heating. This type of well-built pit is rarely found in the region, lending support to the notion that local resources were processed at this settlement.

Both Site 630 and Site 639 date to the thirteenth century, toward the end of the Payson area's prehistoric habitation. Both are located in the uplands away from the creek zone, and both have three-sided structures. At Site 630, a subrectangular room (number 2) seems to have served as the main habitation room for the family or task group that lived there, and the two three-sided rooms (numbers 1 and 3) seem to have been specialized-use structures that were sequentially occupied. These conclusions are based on the supposition that three-sided structures served as auxiliary buildings used on a part-time basis for specialized activities. At Site 639, however, the three-sided room is clearly the main structure, and the artifacts found in it indicate a full range of habitation activities. Thus, evidence from neighboring sites indicates that the shape of a structure does not correlate in a simple manner with the function of a structure. We will return to this important issue as we discuss further evidence.

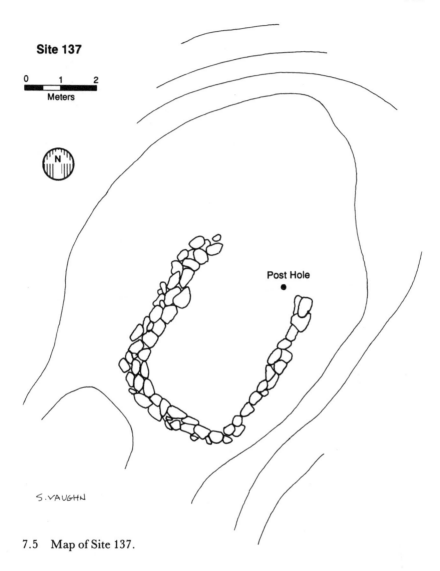

Site 137

0   1   2
Meters

N

Post Hole
•

S.VAUGHN

7.5   Map of Site 137.

Throughout both the Payson and Star Valley areas there are even simpler sites that have only a single structure, often accompanied by a scatter of artifacts or an occasional concentrated midden. Sites 137 and 138 are located near each other on a ridge in the upland zone. Site 137 (Fig. 7.5) consists of a three-sided structure that the excavator suggests was used as a temporary shelter for wild plant gathering activities

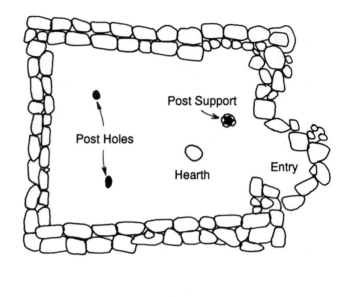

Site 138

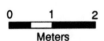

Meters

7.6   Map of Site 138.

(Montero 1988). The structure is quite small, enclosing only 7 m² of floor area and opening to the north. The only floor feature discovered was a single posthole near the open end of the structure. From the absence of a hearth and the northfacing opening, we can infer that if the occupation was short-term, as we expect, it would most likely have occurred during the warm summer months.

Site 138 (Fig. 7.6) consists of a more substantially built four-sided rectangular structure with a doorway opening to the east. Inside the room were a hearth and three postholes. From the rubble wall fall, it appears as if the walls may have been nearly full-height masonry. This is a far more substantial building than that at Site 137, enclosing almost 16 m² of floor area. Although the construction of the building and the somewhat greater abundance of artifacts present at Site 138 indicate a longer-term occupation than at Site 137, we still believe that sites like these were only seasonally occupied, although possibly on a recurring basis.

Rock Shelters

Although almost all settlement in the Payson area was in the open, most often on ridge tops, a few small sites were located in rock shelters, which were naturally formed by the large granite boulders that occur in pockets across the entire region. In our investigations, we examined several rock shelter sites on land parcels near Payson; none were found in the area around Star Valley. Most exhibited short-term occupations that date to the period of maximum population in the region.

One rock shelter site yielded evidence for a surprisingly long occupation span that may have begun as early as the Archaic period and continued intermittently to early historic times. The Horton Rock Shelter site (Fig. 7.7) is situated in a small sheltered area formed by large granite boulders and includes the area in front of the shelter (Hohmann 1988c). The site is located along the side of Horton Canyon adjacent to a permanent spring that probably offered a ready water supply for both humans and animals. The canyon encloses a small alluvial valley that would have provided arable land for cultivation. As is the case with most cave and rock shelter sites, repeated occupation of the same area has resulted in a compressed and often mixed stratigraphy of cultural deposits and features. The artifacts that were recovered implied that some habitation or use of the · site occurred during four periods: pre-A.D. 600, A.D. 800–1000, A.D. 1150–1275, and A.D. 1850–1910 (Hohmann 1988c:22). A potentially problematic radiocarbon date indicates that some activities took place at the site in the late sixteenth century; if this is accurate, it would be the earliest evidence of Apache habitation in the region. It is likely that only one or a few families occupied the site at any one time and that during more prosperous times most of the local inhabitants lived in a larger village nearby, such as Site 164. Tonto National Forest survey records indicate that Site 164 was a village dating to roughly A.D. 800–1000. Even with Horton Canyon's favorable geographic

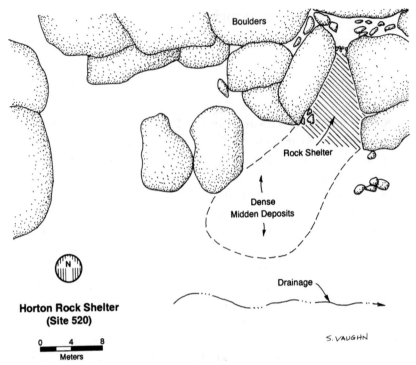

7.7   Map of Horton Rock Shelter Complex.

setting, the rock shelter there—as is the case with others we have found—seems to have played only a minor role in the total settlement system.

The other rock shelter sites found in the Payson area are often associated with bedrock mortars and metates. This suggests that a small task or family group established itself in an expedient shelter—away from its home base—in order to procure and process some of the ripening pinyon nuts or other wild seeds and nuts that grew in the region. In shelters where habitation remains were found, the residues were always minimal, indicating a very short-term occupation.

Mini-Hamlets or Reoccupied Household Communities

Some of the small sites we investigated consisted of more than individual structures and, instead, resembled mini-hamlets. This type of site stemmed from two different situations: first, where the geographic setting was favorable, small groups would reoccupy the same site, build new structures, and leave the remains of more structures than were occupied at any one time; second, small groups would occupy all of the rooms simultaneously, forming a settlement that was larger than a typical household community but not as large as a hamlet.

We believe that Site 648 (Figs. 7.8 and 7.9) is an example of a reoccupied household community, manifesting examples of almost every variety of structure we have defined at other small sites. Site 648 is situated on top of a high narrow ridge overlooking Houston Creek. Its residents had ready access to the arable land in the creek zone and complementary resources in the upland zone. Although the stratigraphic evidence is quite complex and the artifacts found in each building add to the complexity, we believe that Site 648 experienced two major building phases (Lindauer 1991f). The earliest structures appear to be two free-standing subrectangular rooms (3 and 4). Both are large (22 m² and 17 m², respectively) and face each other across a small flat area that may have served as a plaza. Although disturbance by plant roots and pothunters have kept us from identifying any coherent floor features, the size and heavy construction of the rooms indicate that they were used for habitation. Furthermore, the artifact density at the site provides additional evidence that the occupation was probably long-term, perhaps year-round. Associated with rooms 3 and 4 were several open-ended structures that served to enclose the plaza area. Two of these (5 and 6) could be described as examples of three-sided structures. Altogether, rooms 3, 4, 5, and 6 constitute a compact, orderly settlement with two habitation rooms and several open structures, all enclosing a small, open outdoor space on top of a high ridge with sweeping views of the countryside.

Only a meter from the western edge of room 3 was a large rectangular structure composed of two rooms (numbers 1 and 2). Like rooms 3 and 4, these had substantial masonry walls that were at least half-height, if not full-height. Both rooms were large, with more than 22 m² of floor area each. The walls were very neatly built in a single construction episode in which the outside wall was built first and then a lighter partition wall was erected inside. The construction is similar to the last construction phase at Site 620 and could easily be interpreted as a later-

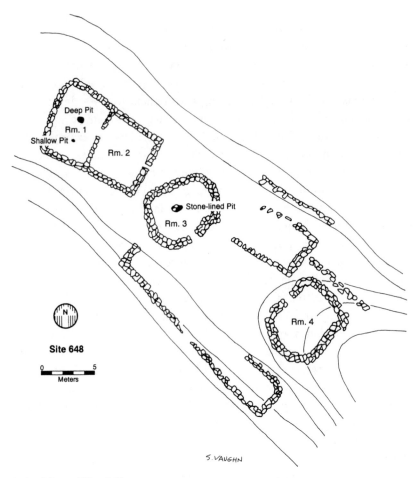

7.8   Map of Site 648.

period structure, except for the fact that its entrance is largely obstructed by room 3, which appears, based on its subrectangular shape, to have been constructed earlier. If rooms 1 and 2 do prove to be later structures, their strange orientation might be attributed to the fact that room 3 offered protection from the strong winds that sweep the ridge top. Thus, their closeness to room 3 might have been seen as an advantage by its prehistoric inhabitants. Of particular interest is the effort and precise workmanship that went into constructing the rooms in each of the site's two phases. The walls are as well constructed as

7.9 View of Site 648 with subrectangular rooms and plaza in foreground and two rectangular rooms in background.

those found at larger villages, indicating a real commitment to this community.

It is difficult to generalize about household communities because they exhibit a wide range of variability. They are, by far, most numerous during the A.D. 1000–1300 period and, as far as the current evidence shows, their residents subsisted on a balanced diet of domestic and wild plants and hunted animals. They engaged in a variety of domestic activities; rarely is there any indication that they were involved in highly specialized activities. Rather, these household communities are the elemental components of the flexible settlement system that I argue characterized the Payson-Star Valley area, and probably much of the American Southwest, prehistorically. This is not to ignore the existence of sites that are more specialized. There are small sites that consist of check dams, lithic quarries, bedrock mortars, and isolated roasting pits. Clearly, these are not settlements but special activity sites away from settlements. What is informative is the apparently low number of special activities sites, which is far less than the number of small household community sites. The conclusion we must draw is that the people of Payson-Star Valley conducted most of their daily tasks in close geographic proximity to their settlements. Instead of ranging out from their residential communities to hunt, farm, or procure materials, they tended to establish their residences close to necessary resources.

8

□ *Tools of the Past:*

□ *The Material Inventory*

□ *of Prehistoric Payson*

Although it is the baffling diversity of building traditions that distinguishes the prehistoric occupants of the Payson region as needing further study, it is their material inventory that provides the data for most analyses of cultural affiliation or achievement. These are the articles of everyday life that were used for the procurement, preparation, and storage of food and for the manufacture of other necessities of life. It includes, too, objects that have ceremonial or religious significance and items that were used as parts of clothing or simply as toys. We generally refer to any object that has been made by humans as an artifact, whether it was intended for utilitarian, ceremonial, or frivolous pursuits.

Because their physical properties aid their preservation, artifacts made of stone or fired clay are by far the most numerous in the archaeological record. Although there may have been objects that were made of organic materials, such as wood, fibers, or skins, which are now absent, the archaeologist can still go a long way toward reconstructing the inventory used in antiquity from the remains of stone, ceramic, and other inorganic materials that are preserved for us today. Our clearest picture, though, will be of activities that involved the use of objects made from durable materials, while those activities that involved only perishable materials, or few material objects, will present greater difficulties in reconstruction. Nevertheless, through careful study of the context and the nature of the objects, we can develop some insights into most aspects of past life.

The majority of artifacts discussed in this chapter were recovered during the excavations at Shoofly Village, although many of the pieces were found at hamlet and household community sites. The assemblage from each site is in some way unique, yet overall there is a great similarity among the implements used by the people of all the Payson settlements, particularly during the height of their occupation around A.D. 1100–1200. It is our purpose both to describe the shared inventory of artifacts and to note the differences that might be related to specialized activities, different time periods, and external contacts.

The information presented here is derived from a variety of studies by members of our staff and archaeologists from the Tonto National Forest. More specifically, I have drawn on Wood (1987), Lindauer (1991a), Simon (1988), Simon and Burton (1991), and Duennwald (1986) for data on local ceramics and on Bradley (1991a) and Stone and Bradley (1991) for data on stone tools. Considering that our project alone has analyzed more than 500,000 objects, it is clear that many other individuals have also made contributions.

A presentation of detailed counts of each artifact type from each excavation location is well beyond the scope of this volume. Nevertheless, I think it is important for the reader to recognize that, although artifacts are present in almost every locality within an archaeological site, the number of artifacts and the relative frequency of artifact types vary widely. As archaeologists, we use this information to tell us about patterns of artifact discard, associations between artifacts that were used together, and the location of specific activities within a settlement.

Table 8.1 provides a summary of artifact counts by class of material for each room where significant excavations took place at Shoofly Village. About half of the artifacts tabulated by our project were recovered from rooms. The other half were recovered from plazas, outside midden areas, and open spaces associated with the settlement and are not included in the table.[1] The table shows that, in every room excavated, ceramics are more frequent than lithic pieces, usually several times

Table 8.1   Total Number and Percentages of Lithics, Ceramics, and
Groundstone Removed from Excavated Rooms at Shoofly Village.

	Lithics		Ceramics		Groundstone	
Room	Count	% of Total	Count	% of Total	Count	% of Total
1	404	0.90	4,079	1.79	8	1.08
3	1,424	3.17	10,645	4.68	19	2.55
5	987	2.19	12,128	5.33	20	2.69
6	149	0.33	1,096	0.48	1	0.13
7	1,678	3.73	10,202	4.48	67	9.01
21	1,995	4.43	12,568	5.52	73	9.81
22	778	1.73	4,889	2.15	11	1.48
30	309	0.69	523	0.23	12	1.61
31	1,273	2.83	3,676	1.62	20	2.69
32	514	1.14	2,844	1.25	17	2.28
41	6,786	15.08	25,544	11.22	107	14.38
50	1,644	3.65	6,307	2.77	32	4.30
51	1,410	3.13	3,433	1.51	32	4.30
52	1,213	2.70	6,469	2.84	41	5.51
53	604	1.34	1,931	0.85	8	1.08
61	412	0.92	2,387	1.05	6	0.81
Totals	21,580	47.97	108,721	47.78	474	63.71

more frequent. One should remember, however, that the ceramics are fragmentary pieces that, despite their large numbers, probably represent only five to fifteen vessels in each room.

It is also noteworthy that some rooms have far more artifacts than other rooms. Room 41 is an excellent example of high artifact counts. As we discussed in Chapter 5, we believe this reflects both its long occupation over multiple time periods and its use as a receptacle for trash after it was abandoned.

More detailed analyses of the forms of ceramic vessels, lithic tools, and groundstone implements allow us to hypothesize about the kinds of activities that took place in a room, while mineralogical and chemical analyses often reveal the locations where specific artifacts were manufactured.

Ceramics as Containers

Ceramics are by far the most abundant material recovered in the excavation of Payson area sites. We expect that ceramics were used in a wide variety of prehistoric activities and, hence, can provide us with a broad spectrum of information. Over 98 percent of the ceramics from our excavations are plainware pieces. Plainware ceramics are those that have no decorative features. The majority of potsherds throughout the Southwest, and in most areas of the world, are plainwares, although their decorated counterparts receive most of the attention in analysis and publication. Our own chemical and petrographic studies indicate that most of the plainware sherds were produced locally, while none of the decorated pieces found in our excavations were manufactured in the immediate vicinity.

The plainware ceramics found at Shoofly Village and elsewhere in the Payson-Star Valley region are part of what archaeologists have designated as the Central Arizona Plainware series (Wood 1987). This category includes a large group of brownwares and some redwares that are difficult to separate into subtypes on the basis of appearance alone. Archaeologists have relied most heavily on the distinct inclusions in the clay to differentiate subtypes from one another. This is based on the assumption that tempering material or clay containing specific minerals would be selected by a prehistoric potter for its particular qualities or its availability and that these choices would vary among potters who came from different groups.

Tonto Plain, the most common subtype of Central Arizona Plainware in our collection, has some form of crushed granite as the predominant inclusion. This appears in the clay body as quartz and feldspar fragments with differing amounts and types of mica and black minerals, such as hornblende and pyroxene. The differences in the proportion of these minerals, which are the main constituents of granite, have allowed archaeologists to separate Tonto Plain into at least three varieties: Tonto, Verde, and Verde-Payson.

Whether the observed differences in mineral inclusions are a result of purposeful selection by the potter to create vessels with different functional or aesthetic qualities, or whether they are the result of the variation that occurs naturally in many clays is a major question that our project is seeking to answer with further field and laboratory studies. As a first step, samples of clays and rocks from the Payson region have been collected and their constituents analyzed (Burton 1991). In addition, vessel fragments found in excavations have been examined in an attempt to discover a relationship between the apparent function of a vessel type and the kinds of temper or clays used (Simon 1988; Simon and Burton 1991).

Among ceramic vessels whose shape could be identified, the most common were jars (Fig. 8.1 C,D), although many others could be considered bowls (Fig. 8.1 A). Jars varied widely in their volume and in the size of their mouth opening. This was particularly important because the relationship between jar volume and orifice size indicates whether a vessel could be used more efficiently for food preparation or for storage. Duennwald (1986) in her study of Shoofly Village ceramics found that many of the vessel forms were intermediate between what has traditionally been defined as a bowl shape and a jar shape (Fig. 8.1 B). In Simon and Burton's study (1991) of pottery from Star Valley, the majority of rim and neck sherds could not be assigned with certainty to bowl or jar categories, further confirming the existence of an intermediate vessel form. Although examples of the full range of Southwestern plainware vessel shapes were found in the Payson-Star Valley assemblages, it is interesting to note that the majority of sherds were most accurately identified as belonging to a special, potentially multiple-use vessel category. This category could be called either a deep bowl or an open-mouthed jar. The vessels might have functioned as general utility vessels for food preparation and may have been particularly practical in households with limited numbers of vessels. If this inference holds up to further testing, it will lend support to my hypothesis about the flexibility exhibited by the people of this region in addressing their needs.

Some of the vessels recovered from excavations have a red slip on the exterior and/or a carbon coating on the interior. These treatments definitely had aesthetic value; they would also tend to provide the vessels with an impermeable surface, especially when they were burnished. This might be important if the storage of liquid or semiliquid substances was common. Simon and Burton (1991) also noted that, over time, jars, in particular, appear to have been made so that they would have greater hardness and lower porosity. This seems to have been

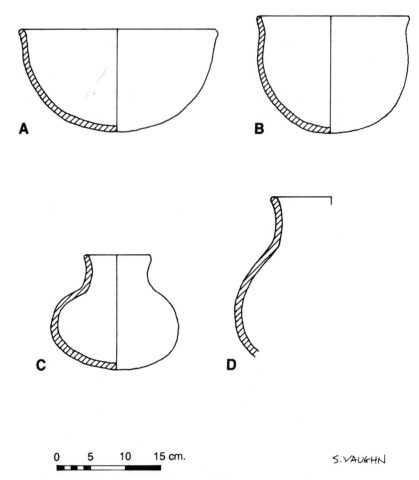

S.VAUGHN

8.1   Profiles of common ceramic vessel shapes.

accomplished by using a coarse temper in the clay, an addition that would also aid in the successful firing of the pots.

Not surprisingly, the greatest diversity of vessel shapes occurred at the largest sites (Lindauer 1991a). This further supports our contention that all of the primary villages and almost all of the hamlets were year-round settlements housing multiple families who carried out the full range of domestic activities. Among the smaller household community sites, those in the creek zone had the greatest ceramic diversity, with both storage and serving pieces well represented. Interestingly, most of the upland sites had fewer vessel types represented, with storage jars predominating. Serving bowls were found at only two upland sites. Our interpretation is that at least a basic suite of vessels for storage, preparation, and food serving activities were in use at almost every significant site, but the short occupation span of some sites might have diminished the likelihood of finding certain vessels there unless they accidently broke.

Potsherds from vessels obviously manufactured outside the Payson-Star Valley area also were found at all village and hamlet sites and at many household sites as well. Our current understanding is that all ceramic material exhibiting painted decoration was manufactured elsewhere, usually at a substantial distance, and brought into the region. Two lines of evidence are used to pinpoint the location of manufacture of a variety of ceramics. The traditional method has been to identify the location where a particular decorative style is most common and most developed. In recent years scientific methods have been used increasingly to characterize the minerals and chemical elements that occur in the clay, temper, and paint, allowing geologists to trace the location of these raw materials and, therefore, the most likely area of manufacture. In the absence of painted decoration, one must rely on scientific analyses to identify the origin of plainwares. Our petrographic analysis indicates that, although a modest proportion of the plainware inventory may have come from outside the region, the majority of plainwares were made in the Payson-Star Valley area.

We find that virtually all plainware ceramics that we have identified by petrography and vessel appearance to have been made in the general area appear to have been constructed by a "paddle and anvil" technique. This technique involves shaping a vessel out of a lump of clay with two flat implements and contrasts with the "coil and scrape" technique. The paddle and anvil technique appears to be most closely associated with the desert lowlands of Arizona and the Hohokam. This parallels other evidence we have that the early settlements of the Payson region maintained some links to the south. What is surprising is that the paddle and anvil technique dominates the Payson inventory throughout all of its phases, even after A.D. 1100 when evidence of decorated ceramics indicates increasing contact with the north and east—areas where a coil and scrape technique predominates. Rather than pointing to influences from one direction or another, this may reflect the fact that the industries and people of the Payson region may be more autonomous than we normally expect of prehistoric groups.

The usual assumption by archaeologists is that decorated ceramics are brought into a region as containers for goods or as trade goods themselves. Because the decorated ceramics found at Shoofly Village and other sites in the region occurred only as small pieces of pottery, we examined the possibility that they came into the area as potsherds rather than as whole vessels (Lindauer 1991b). We found, in fact, that the average size of decorated sherds was half that of plainware sherds. Furthermore, no whole decorated vessels were recovered, while numerous whole or largely reconstructible plainware vessels were found. This has led us to speculate that most, if not all, painted ceramics entered the Payson area not as whole vessels, but as fragments! This still could mean that they came as trade goods, but as trinkets rather than as containers. It could also mean that they were not objects of trade but were collected as souvenirs by people from Payson who traveled to places where this pottery was manufactured or where it was used and the broken pieces were scattered on the ground.

There are two important implications to be drawn from this observation, if it continues to prove true. First, the people of the Payson area may not have been active in long-distance, interregional trade, at least insofar as it included decorated vessels. Second, the common archaeological practice of ceramic cross-dating for determining the age of a local deposit based on the known age of a trade ware would have to be adjusted to recognize this unusual manner of obtaining foreign pottery.

Lindauer (1991b) examined the second implication, a reevaluation of ceramic cross-dating, by comparing our radiocarbon dates with the widely accepted dates of manufacture for decorated sherds found at our sites. There is a substantial overlap in the two sets of dates, but Lindauer's conclusion was that the radiocarbon dates tended to be somewhat later than the generally accepted manufacturing date. Thus, ceramic cross-dating has the effect of making our sites appear to be up to a century earlier than radiocarbon dates indicate. Our investigation of this phenomenon is not conclusive due to the limited number of radiocarbon dates and decorated sherds, but our results suggest that our hypothesis about the origin of decorated sherds may be correct and that it should be considered a possibility in other circumstances.

Although the quantity of decorated sherds is small, the range of decorated types is surprising. These types indicate that material entered the Payson area settlements from many different locations across Arizona. It is a standard archaeological assumption that the presence of a nonlocal sherd at a site indicates some form of contact with the originating location. As we have discussed above, our own study of decorated sherd size and its possible implications for the mode of procurement injects some uncertainty into this basic assumption. Moreover, we believe that this may not be solely a Payson phenomenon but may represent a process at work in many regions of the world.

Whether or not decorated sherds entered Payson as containers, as sherds that were items of purposeful trade, or as trinkets collected by the local residents while on their own travels, some form of interaction between the regions in question is indicated. The nature of this interaction may have been quite different in each case. For example, trinket collectors may have visited the producing region when its settlements were no longer occupied and, hence, may not have had any culturally significant interaction with the people. Another possibility is that the ceramics did not come to Payson directly from the source locations but first were taken to an intermediary settlement, perhaps as trade goods, where they were used, broken, and then fragments were eventually carried to Payson. This would suggest that Payson residents were in contact with fewer localities across the region than is implied by the diversity of the nonlocal ceramics. We are working on ways to differentiate among these possible situations, but for the moment we will sidestep the issue by accepting the presence of intrusive sherds as evidence of some interaction with external areas in the general direction the sherds came from, but perhaps not with the source areas themselves.

Given the natural routes of communication leading out of the Payson area, it is possible to identify four major areas of prehistoric settlement bordering the Payson-Star Valley area, each with its own decorated ceramic tradition (Fig. 8.2). To the north and northeast on the Colorado Plateau is where Little Colorado whitewares and Tusayan whitewares were made. To the east is the area where Mogollon and Cibola whitewares and brownwares originated. To the southeast in the Tonto

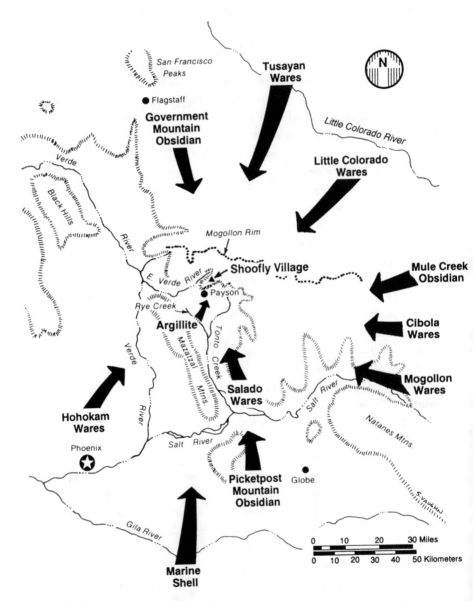

8.2   Map of hypothesized locations where decorated ceramics and exotic raw materials found at Shoofly Village originated.

Basin and beyond is where Salado redwares and Tonto corrugated wares were made. To the south and southwest are the Hohokam lowlands with their red-on-buff wares and Gila plainware. One should also recognize that, once decorated ceramics were brought into the Payson area, their distribution to specific settlements may have been quite complicated. Two possible scenarios are a situation where material came from a particular region during one period but not during another, and a situation where material from a particular region entered the Payson area over a long time but was brought only to certain settlements.

In general, the Hohokam buffwares that have been found in our project area are relatively early, dating to about A.D. 600–1000, and their distribution is very limited. Among the primary villages examined, Mayfield Canyon, Round Valley, and Risser Ranch yielded a few buffwares in surface collections. Surprisingly, Shoofly Village had no evidence of Hohokam material, perhaps reflecting its northerly location or the possibility that it intentionally isolated itself from activities to the south. Among the hamlets we excavated in the region, only Scorpion Rock Ruin had buffwares and these most likely were associated its early pithouse component. In fact, most of the sites that contained buffwares appeared to be small pithouse communities (Sites 491, 21, 520, and 650) that predate the major Payson phase occupation in the region. None of these small sites resemble the typical ridge-top household community that we believe characterized the Payson settlement system at its zenith. We would also guess that the buffwares found at large village sites are actually from earlier pithouse components at the site, rather than the result of Hohokam interaction with the later village settlement.

Pottery sherds from Tonto Basin to the south are relatively common at many of the hamlet and village sites, but they are not the later well-known Tonto polychrome wares. Instead, the Tonto pottery that is found throughout the Payson area at sites from many periods consists of Salado red, Tonto corrugated, and Tonto plainware. The famous Tonto Basin polychromes were produced only at the end of the thirteenth century, when most, if not all, of the sites in the Payson area were already abandoned. Most of the Tonto material in our collections came from sites to the east, in the vicinity of Star Valley, suggesting that the favored route of travel followed Houston Creek down to Tonto Creek rather than the route of modern State Highway 87, which heads directly south from Payson. Recognition of the existence of this route also opens the possibility that the Hohokam buffwares found in our study area came via the Tonto Basin.

Because of the similarity between the locally produced brownwares and the Mogollon plainware tradition, as well as the presence of Cibola whitewares, we assume that substantial contact existed with settlements to the east, all the way to the White Mountains and possibly beyond. At the same time there is evidence of contact with the north in the form of Little Colorado whitewares. Both directions appear to be potentially important for interaction with other culture areas by prehistoric Payson-area people. While it is difficult to base sweeping conclusions on a small number of sherds, we believe that by the thirteenth century the primary direction of cross-cultural contact was to the north, with evidence of decreasing interaction with societies to the east.

The overall picture is of widely spread production locations for the decorated ceramics found in our study area. Despite recognition that the presence of these sherds may not indicate direct cultural contact with outside areas, we believe that the situation still suggests that the people of Payson participated in changing "spheres of influence." Early on, influences emanated mainly from the southwest, later changed to the east and north, and finally came chiefly from the north. Throughout this time, contact with the Tonto Basin region in the south appears to have continued; perhaps some of the other intrusive potsherds we have found in our excavations reached Payson via the Tonto Basin.

Chipped Stone Tools

Most of the prehistoric tools from the Payson area are chipped stone tools. Some were made with as simple a technology as knocking two stones together in order to break one in such a way that a sharp cutting edge was created. Others were made with a more sophisticated technology in which specialized tools were used to carefully remove flakes, resulting in the finely crafted and amazingly small projectile points of the Payson area. Raw material for chipped stone implements is widely available in the Mogollon Rim countryside due to the erosion of many exposed geological strata. The most prized local materials were flints and cherts, but quartzite, basalt, and schist were also employed.

In addition to the locally available raw materials, modest quantities of obsidian, a volcanic glass, were obtained from several distant areas (see Fig. 8.2). X-ray fluorescence analysis of obsidian fragments from Shoofly Village indicated that more than 60 percent came from Government Mountain near Flagstaff, 26 percent from Picketpost Mountain near Superior, and the remainder from Mule Creek/Gwynn Canyon in west-central New Mexico (Shackley 1986). It seems unlikely that people from Shoofly Village would have traveled regularly to these distant locations to secure lithic raw materials. It is possible that they incidentally collected obsidian while they traveled to hunt animals or gather plant resources. The archaeological evidence, however, indicates that none of the foods found at Payson-area sites would have required travel to these distant locations (see Chapter 9). I hypothesize that obsidian reached the Payson area through trade with mobile middlemen or through "down-the-line" exchange from one community to the next (see Renfrew 1975 for a discussion of alternate means of obsidian movement). Another possibility is that obsidian reached Shoofly Village and other Payson-Star Valley sites as trinkets, just as we have hypothesized for decorated potsherds.

The laboratory analysis of chipped stone found during the project focused on identifying what types of tools were present, and then examining in more detail selected categories, such as projectile points (Fig. 8.3) (Bradley 1991a; Stone and Bradley 1991). Overall, the chipped stone tools from Payson-Star Valley sites appear to have been made by many different individuals as an immediate response to their needs. This type of expedient production does not result in carefully crafted or consistently shaped tools. Although most of the pieces had reasonably effective cutting, scraping, or piercing qualities, their shape bore little consistent relationship to the raw material selected, reinforcing the expedient nature of production. By contrast, projectile points and a limited number of other retouched tools exhibited a far more regular and controlled approach to manufacture. These tools may have been produced by a more limited number of craft specialists, as this required a mastery of pressure flaking techniques.

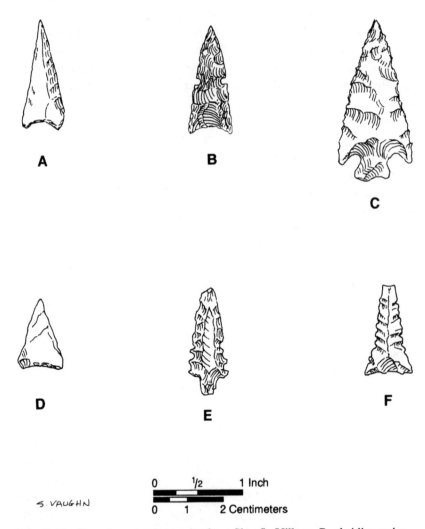

S. VAUGHN

```
0        ½           1 Inch
0        1           2 Centimeters
```

8.3   Projectile points: A, chert point from Shoofly Village; B, obsidian point from Shoofly Village; C, chert point from Site 532, D, chert point from Shoofly Village; E, chert point from site 532; F, chert point from Shoofly Village.

Not surprising for a basically expedient industry, the most common lithic form recovered from most sites was shatter. Shatter refers to the chunkier pieces of stone produced by hitting rocks together. This material accounted for over half of the pieces at some sites, and as low as 20 percent at other sites. Shatter may have been the first step toward a more refined tool, but sometimes even the most irregular shatter was found to have been utilized as a tool. Tertiary flakes, which are relatively slender pieces of stone without traces of cortex, were the next most common category. Primary and secondary flakes, which are defined by the amount of visible cortex, followed in frequency. All of the flake categories included pieces that would have served well for many uses. Cores made up less than 10 percent of the stone assemblage at each site. At most sites the proportion of different lithic forms would have been within the range of that produced from tool manufacture, an observation consistent with an expedient approach to production. A major divergence from this pattern occurred at several upland sites where the amount of shatter was relatively low, indicating that more tools were brought to the site already made and fewer were manufactured there.

Of the pieces that were found to have traces of the kind of wear that indicates they were actually used, flakes accounted for two-thirds, shatter about a quarter, and the rest consisted of cores, tabular pieces, and irregular shapes. Of the utilized flakes, one-fourth exhibited deliberate retouch that prepared an edge for use and/or shaped the tool. The remainder of the flakes and all of the shatter exhibited evidence of having been used as they were first produced, without further modification. The proportion of flakes that were retouched (one-quarter) is actually quite high for a lithic assemblage in the prehistoric Southwest, indicating a relatively high level of concern among the people of Payson for the manufacture of effective stone tools.

Following the work of others in the Southwest, we assume that stone tools with low-angle, sharp working edges were probably used for cutting and slicing, while pieces with high-angle, blunt working edges were used for scraping and, possibly, sawing (Nelson 1981; Wilmsen 1968). Most of the creek zone sites had tools with the full range of edge angles, reflecting a diversity of both plant and animal procurement and processing activities. By contrast, a few of the upland zone sites had a preponderance of low-angled pieces, implying animal procurement and meat processing activities. At some of the upland sites, such as Site 639, there was also a high number of projectile points, further supporting our inference.

More than 300 projectile points were recovered from excavations at Shoofly Village and about twice that number from other sites investigated in the Payson-Star Valley region (Stone and Bradley 1991). Although nine different point types were defined on the basis of shape, 90 percent of the assemblage consisted of triangular-shaped points (Fig. 8.3A, B, D, F). Of these, the most common type was a small, straight-sided variety, often about 2 cm in length. Next in frequency was a similarly shaped point with side notches, which presumably aided in hafting the point to a shaft. The most commonly used material for all point types was chert (79 percent), followed by basalt (14 percent), and obsidian (6 percent).

Unlike some regions where projectile points can be used for dating sites, the major Payson-area projectile point types do not seem to be particularly sensitive to short-term chronological change (the piece illustrated as Figure 8.3C is from an earlier period). Our own evidence indicates that the same types were in use at virtually all excavated sites that span the period from A.D. 1000 to A.D. 1300. Small triangular points, both side-notched (Fig. 8.3B) and plain (Fig. 8.3A), have also been found at sites in other regions. They resemble points from the Tanque Verde phase (A.D. 1200–1300) in the Tucson Basin; the Canyon Creek phase (A.D. 1325–1400) at Point of Pines in Mogollon territory; and Grasshopper Pueblo during the fourteenth century (Stone and Bradley 1991). These sites, particularly the Mogollon sites, seem to have been inhabited later than Shoofly or other sites in the Payson region. Moreover, the relative number of projectile points recovered from the Payson region is quite high when compared with other shaped stone tools in the local inventory. One possible inference is that hunting game with projectile points was more important for the diet, or more organized in its pursuit, in this area than in neighboring areas. A second inference is that the nature of hunting activities represented by the projectile points developed earlier in the Payson/Star Valley region and was adopted later in regions to the east, possibly through the movement of people.

Groundstone Tools

Groundstone artifacts recovered from sites in the Payson region are a diverse category of tools associated with a number of activities, including food processing (milling stones), wood working (axes, shaft straighteners), house maintenance (floor polishers), and pottery production (polishing stones, anvils). They are also associated with esoteric functions that may have been part of ritual activities (palettes) (Stone 1991).

The largest category of groundstone tools in this region is the milling stone, reflecting the importance of processing plant materials for food. Although the mortars and pestles that are often associated with wild seed and nut processing are present, particularly at some of the small sites, they form a very small proportion of the total assemblage, reflecting the modest role of wild seeds and nuts in the diet. Far more numerous are the manos and metates presumably used in the grinding of large-seeded grains, such as corn. This further confirms the central importance of corn in the diet of people at both large and small sites throughout the Payson-Star Valley region.

Interestingly, among the milling stones there are roughly equal numbers of what would be considered, based on size, one-handed and two-handed manos (Stone 1991). According to Stone and others, one logical inference is that the one-handed mano was a more versatile implement that could be used on a variety of metates and with various seeds. The two-handed mano, however, would have been more a specialized implement presumably designed for use on a larger, flatter metate, and would have become more common as reliance on corn as a food source increased. The variously sized manos indicate the presence of a diversity of food processing activities.

Although they were not common, groundstone axes did occur at a number of sites. The axes were made of fine-grained stone from both local and distant sources, and all of them showed evidence of being hafted to a handle (Fig. 8.4D). We expect that the primary function of these implements was tree cutting and coarse woodworking. In the course of these activities, it would have been easy to break or lose the implement at a distance from the site, and unless it was brought back to be resharpened or discarded at home, we would probably not find it at a

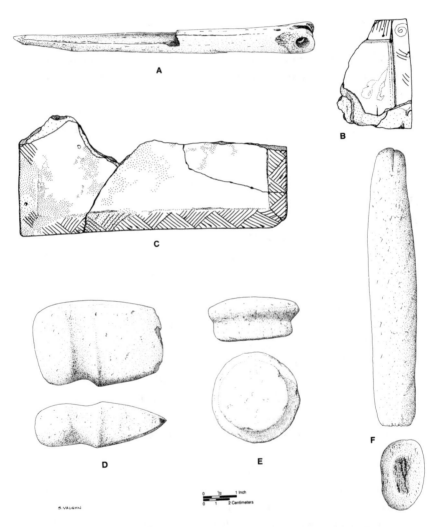

8.4   Bone awl and groundstone implements: A, bone awl from Shoofly
Village; B, stone palette from Site 620; C, stone palette from Site 21; D,
polished stone axe from Site 620; E, basalt anvil stone from Site 634, Star
Valley; F, groundstone pestle from Site 641, Star Valley.

habitation site. Consequently, one could expect axes to be seriously underrepresented in excavations of settlements.

Other groundstone implements were also present in small numbers, but some were significant in the activities they reflected. Small circular handstones with a groove around their edge (Fig. 8.4E) were recovered from several sites, among them Shoofly Village. These are generally interpreted as anvils used in the paddle-and-anvil approach to pottery manufacture. Their presence indicates that pottery production took place at these sites, supporting our findings from the petrographic study of sherds. Flat palettes of fine-grained phyllite schist (Fig. 8.4B,C), best known from their occurrence at Hohokam sites in the Salt-Gila Valley, are believed to have been used to grind pigments, which may have been used for body paint in ceremonial activities. Our project recovered fragmentary palettes from Site 620, Site 21 (collected by local resident), Site 491, and Site 532. Except for Site 620, these sites yielded other Hohokam remains, such as red-on-buff decorated sherds, Gila plainwares, and Hohokam-like pithouse structures (at Site 491 and Site 532).

It is generally believed that the Hohokam cultural traits found at a few sites in the Payson-Star Valley area came from an exchange of ideas and goods, rather than from the actual presence of people from the desert river valleys. Based on the accepted Hohokam chronology, the period of greatest contact between the Payson-Star Valley area and the Hohokam people of the south was about A.D. 850–1000, or Wood's Union Park phase.

These cultural traits, although very rare, have shown up both at hamlet sites (e.g., Site 620) and at household settlements. It appears that Hohokam influence in the region was modest and that it occurred before the period of greatest population growth in Payson. Another interesting fact is that despite the enormous quantity of material recovered from Shoofly Village, no Hohokam material was found there (see discussion of shell in the next section of this chapter). This evidence of Shoofly's isolation from the Hohokam leads us to speculate that the village's interregional connections were primarily to the north and east rather than to the south.

Special Objects

The people of the Payson region utilized a variety of raw materials to manufacture specialized objects that, while not present in large quantities, probably played a substantial role in certain aspects of their lives. Some of these objects served largely utilitarian purposes, such as a tool type we call tabular knives. More than 50 of these relatively large pieces of naturally cleaved schist that has been retouched or battered along at least one edge have been found at Shoofly Village alone. Although similarly shaped tools have sometimes been referred to as "hoes," we believe that they were most likely used in the procurement and preparation of agave (Fish, Fish, and Madsen 1985). These rectangular-shaped tools usually had roughly sharpened edges from 10 to 20 cm long that were used to scrape the fiber out of partially processed agave leaves. It is not clear whether agave was actually cultivated or only collected by the people of this region, nor is it clear how important agave was to the local diet or for producing textile fiber. Because of the nature of its preparation and consumption, evidence for agave use is rare, even if it was commonly used. The fact that agave grows naturally today in various localities of the Payson region, coupled with the fact that the "knives" are ubiquitous throughout the region, leads us to believe that agave was a reasonably important part of the local livelihood.

The people of Payson also worked pieces of bone for use as tools and ornamental objects. At least half of the 50 pieces of worked bone discovered are long, pointed awl-shaped implements that may have been used to process hides and make clothing. All of the awls are made from the shafts of mammal long bones, mostly from deer. One finely preserved awl was purposefully placed in a burial in the cemetery area north of the compound wall at Shoofly Village (Fig. 8.4A). It was over 20 cm long and finely worked to a point at one end. Some of the other pieces of worked bone seemed to have been used as scrapers or were perforated to be used as beads or pendants.

Many of the other specialized objects appear to have served some role in the social and ceremonial life of the community. Their numbers are low, considering the diversity of materials used and the purposes they served. Their rarity may reflect the minor role long-distance trade played in the lives of the people of this region. Over 100 pieces of marine shell, which most likely came from the Gulf of California, were found in all of the excavated areas of Shoofly Village and at some of the smaller sites. The shell, however, was concentrated in the midden areas at Shoofly, particularly in the immediate vicinity of, if not directly associated with, burials. In one case, seven shells were found in a linear arrangement around a burial, suggesting its use as a necklace. The majority of shells were olivella and appeared to have been used as beads or pendants. There were also a few carefully worked shells that appear to have been used as rings or bracelets. It is generally assumed that the Hohokam controlled much of the shell trade in southern Arizona. Since Shoofly lacks other evidence of Hohokam contact, we hypothesize that the shell reached Shoofly through intermediaries.

A relatively soft stone, which we have identified as argillite, was also used for personal decoration. Over 100 worked pieces of this material have been found at Shoofly Village and a few pieces at various other sites in the region. A recent petrographic analysis has identified the primary source of this material as Deer Creek, about 30 km south of Payson at the extreme northern end of the Tonto Basin (Elson and Gundersen 1992). One of the assayed pieces from Shoofly appears to have come from the Del Rio source in the Upper Verde River valley. Most of the argillite objects consisted of flat pendants or beads (Fig. 8.5C–F). Some were made into what appears to have been a ring (Fig. 8.5G). Others were shaped, but not into anything easily identifiable. A few larger pieces of argillite were fashioned into the shape of a small axe. It is possible that these were used for some special purpose. The soft nature of the stone indicates that a ceremonial function is likely because it would not function well for cutting or most other utilitarian activities.

Among the distinctive items found at Shoofly Village are quartz crystals (Fig. 8.5J–K). More than 50 have been found. It is likely that they came from outcrops below Diamond Point Rim about 10 km to the northeast of the site. These crystals have a jewel-like appearance and may have been a valued possession of many of Shoofly's inhabitants. A few appear to have traces of use or battering along one edge, but the majority seem to have been collected for their appearance, rather than as potential tools.

Other minerals have also been recovered in our excavations. Among them are numerous pieces of turquoise or malachite that appear largely to have been shaped into beads, and a few pieces of ochre that probably was used as a pigment.

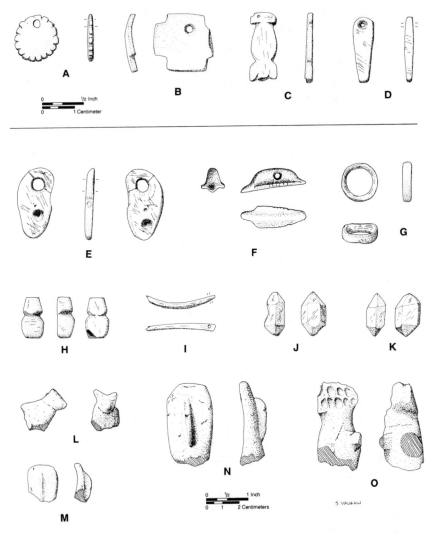

8.5   Small objects from Shoofly Village: A–B, shell pendants; C–F, argillite pendants; G, argillite ring; H, limestone object; I, shell needle; J–K, quartz crystal; L, clay animal figurine; M–N, clay human face figurine; O, fragment of clay figurine with corn impression.

Small figurines manufactured out of ceramic material also appear to have served a non-utilitarian role in the local lifeways. Two dozen figurine fragments have been found by our project. Although many are too small to identify with certainty, several appear to be animal shapes (Fig. 8.5L). Some are probably deer figurines made simply by pinching a lump of clay that may have been formed around a wooden stick. Two clear examples of human figurines, similar to those identified as "bean-faced" at other sites (Denten 1985), have also been found (Fig 8.5M–N). Ceramic figurines are common at Southwestern sites, and those found at Shoofly bear resemblances to examples from Hohokam sites. All of the figurines have been found in a fragmentary condition, most in very small fragments. One explanation for this would parallel our suggestion about decorated ceramics, that is, that they were made else-where and were brought only coincidentally into Payson, already in a broken condition.

When looking back at the material inventory of the prehistoric Pay-son-Star Valley area, one is struck by several important trends. First, the people were capable of producing large quantities of goods. Some of it, such as the variety of vessel forms and high quality chert tools, reflects considerable technological skill and forethought. Their products seem to have been very practical, with many ceramic and groundstone forms to help them in essential food-processing activities. Moreover, the so-called non-utilitarian items are also diverse, but most are present in relatively low quantities and a surprisingly large number were recov-ered in very fragmentary condition. I believe that this situation pro-vides us with some valuable insights into the character of life and social interaction in prehistoric Payson. This is a subject I will return to at the end of Chapter 10.

Note

1. Detailed information on the counts and locations of all artifacts from Shoofly Village and other sites reported in this volume is available in a database format on floppy disks from the author.

9

□
□ *Diet and Daily Life in*
□ *Prehistoric Payson*
□

Just as its temperate climate offered people a comfortable place to live year-round, the Payson region fostered a diversity of plant and animal life that provided the subsistence resources necessary for prehistoric life. The regular rainfall and lengthy frost-free season also made agriculture possible, although its success was restricted by the limited distribution of deep soils. For most settlers, this meant a reliance on relatively non-intensive agriculture, supplemented by a variety of naturally occurring food resources. The distinguishing characteristics of a social system in this kind of environmental setting would be small settlement sizes, carefully selected and dispersed habitation locations, and maintenance of group mobility. This mobility would be manifested in regular trips to widely scattered fields, seasonal movement to zones that supported alternative resources, and periodic relocation of settlements to new areas when soil fertility diminished. It is this tendency toward small-scale, mobile communities that characterized the Payson-Star Valley settlement pattern throughout prehistoric and historic times. This book, however, focuses on one period of time, A.D. 1000–1300 when, through personal industry and creative solutions, the people of the Tonto Rim were able to modify this characteristic pattern. By producing and procuring sufficient resources and by instituting adequate social controls, most people in the region were able to live in large communities for a period of several generations.

The information in this chapter comes from a variety of analyses done by members of the ASU research team. In particular, Joanne Miller (1990, 1991) conducted the macrobotanical examination, Michael Gregory (1989, 1991a) the pollen analysis, and David Eshbaugh (1988) and Karen Atwell (Atwell and Eshbaugh 1991) the faunal studies.

Although current analytical methodologies make it difficult to estimate the actual proportional contribution of various food groups to the total prehistoric diet, the single most important observation we have been able to make is the pervasiveness of an agricultural lifeway based primarily on corn cultivation. Other domesticated and wild plant resources were used, but they were less common and were found in fewer localities (see Appendix 3). The Payson-Star Valley area seems to have been a home to mobile groups for most of its occupation, yet from about A.D. 1000 to A.D. 1250 corn agriculturalists in both large and small settlements dominated the landscape.

Although there is no evidence for the use of any of the known North American domesticated animals, such as dogs and turkeys, there are ample remains that attest to the importance of hunting in the lives of the people of the Tonto Rim. As might be expected, deer was the most important meat resource, with cottontail and jack rabbits also making substantial contributions (see Appendix 4).

A question associated with the degree of mobility is the ability of prehistoric groups to store food. If at least some of the sites were long-term, year-round settlements, then we would expect to find evidence for substantial storage. We have recovered a preponderance of jars and jar-like ceramic vessels from both small and large communities, indicating that a reasonable level of storage was present at most settlements. We would, however, expect to find evidence of permanent storage facilities at the larger sites, if they were home to reasonably large populations for sustained periods of time. During our excavations we were able to identify only small, below-ground storage pits. These pits would have provided some storage capacity, but certainly only for small groups. In the few years since our excavations, however, a new type of storage facility has been identified in excavations in nearby Tonto Basin (Lindauer 1992). This is a large, above-ground, mud-and-plant fiber silo that, in at least one well-preserved case, was capable of holding an estimated 55 gallons of stored material. The problem with identifying these silos in the archaeological record, however, is that their mud-and-fiber walls almost always deteriorate and, thus, they are virtually unobservable during excavations. The silos that were preserved in the Tonto Basin were always found to have a circular platform of flat rocks as a foundation. We now hypothesize that such rock platforms represent the prehistoric remains of large storage silos for dried plant foods.

Without knowing their significance, excavators at our Payson sites and at many other sites in the Southwest may have failed to recognize these platforms and, instead, may have recorded them simply as clusters of stone, since they could be easily mistaken for potentially meaningless groupings of rocks. A close reexamination of the notes and photographs from our excavations revealed that, at least at Shoofly Village and Risser Ranch, these types of platforms were present. Hence, we are willing to suggest tentatively that large-scale food storage existed in the large agricultural villages but not necessarily in hamlets or household communities. We would not go so far as to suggest that silos provided centralized storage for a population beyond the community, as we hypothesize for the Tonto Basin, but rather that they provided a degree of insurance against a bad crop for that particular settlement.

Plant Resources

A closer look at the carbonized plant material recovered at Shoofly Village reveals in some detail the subsistence pursuits of its inhabitants (Miller 1990). Maize was the most frequently recovered plant taxa in both the core roomblock and peripheral rooms. In addition, four wild perennial plants—juniper, agave, walnut, and manzanita—and two wild annuals—cheno-am and purslane—were found in both core and peripheral rooms. This attests to a general uniformity of plant use among the occupation units at Shoofly.

Interestingly, however, additional domesticated plants—beans, squash, and cotton—were found in the core roomblock, and maize was more abundant there as well. This may indicate that the first settlers at Shoofly relied on a general subsistence strategy that combined maize cultivation with the consumption of some of the more numerous wild resources of the region. As the community grew, this pattern continued, but reliance on maize cultivation increased, other domesticates were introduced, and selected wild resources, such as cheno-am, came to have economic significance. Hence, the intensification of agriculture that accompanied the establishment of the core roomblock did not lead to a diminished reliance on wild resources. If anything, there was an increased reliance on those wild species that thrived in the disturbed soil surrounding the settlement (i.e., cheno-am and purslane), but also a growth in the inventory of domesticated plants.

By identifying the seasons when these plants would ripen, the archaeologist obtains a rare opportunity to evaluate whether a community was occupied seasonally or year-round. At Shoofly Village there was evidence of tansy mustard, agave, globemallow, and other wild annuals that are available in the spring, and domestic plants and walnuts that are harvested in the fall. Thus, the presence of plant materials representing both of the major growing seasons suggests a year-round occupation of the site. Equally important is the fact that the plants were found both in the peripheral units and in the core, indicating permanent occupation throughout the settlement. Although I find this interpretation reasonable, the reader should be aware that the occupation of the site in the winter is not documented. Since most of the known food resources could be stored for a period of time, the settlement may have been vacated in the winter or inhabited by only a fraction of its normal population, the remainder moving to lower elevations where it would be warmer.

At the Star Valley sites studied by Miller (1991), the botanical evidence indicates that they, too, were settled by simple agriculturalists focused on maize. Maize kernels, which were found in most excavation units, was virtually the only domesticated plant residue recovered. One exception was a site with Hohokam attributes where a bean was identified. Seeds and plant parts from wild species were also recovered from the Star Valley sites but they exhibited less diversity than Shoofly. This pattern was true of the household sites, as well as of the 19-room hamlet, Site 620. Overall, the picture is one of settlement by agriculturalists who practiced a non-intensive regime similar to that of the early residents of Shoofly Village. Given the fact that the settlements in Star Valley are contemporaneous with, and in fact may have existed longer than, the core roomblock at Shoofly, the variation in the agricultural regime should not be interpreted as simply chronological. Rather, it appears that the overall low population density and the relatively small settlement sizes minimized the need to introduce diverse domesticates and intensify production. There is also the possibility that the distinctive dietary patterns of the occupants of Shoofly's core roomblocks were due to their membership in a social group whose customary subsistence pursuits were new to the region, and to the possibility that different groups occupied the sites we investigated in Star Valley.

Miller (1991) also compared the botanical evidence from Shoofly Village with that from two other large prehistoric settlements, Grasshopper and Point of Pines. The study showed an overall similarity in the plant resources used by inhabitants of all three sites. Maize was the primary crop, and it was supplemented with a variety of wild perennials and annuals. Although Shoofly Village was the smallest of the three settlements and was abandoned first, its residents appear to have utilized the broadest range of domesticates and the fewest wild resources. The variety of perennial plants from both Grasshopper and Point of Pines is twice that of Shoofly and reflects the use of many different vegetation zones. This is particularly true of Point of Pines where evidence points to the exploitation of plant resources from relatively distant localities. Both Shoofly's and Grasshopper's inhabitants seem to have stayed closer to home in their harvesting. Given the vagaries of botanical preservation and the archaeological recovery of plant remains, it would be imprudent to draw too detailed a conclusion from this comparison. It does, however, seem justified to suggest that the people of Shoofly Village were at least as effective, if not more so, in their use of domesticated plants as the people living in the larger and later pueblos to the east.

By examining the microscopic pollen grains that are deposited at an archaeological site, it is possible to reconstruct the type of vegetation that surrounded a settlement at the time that the deposits were formed. Michael Gregory has done that for Shoofly Village (1989) and for some of the Star Valley sites (1991a). In both cases, he found that the vegetation surrounding settlements was broadly similar to that today, with several interesting differences. When Shoofly Village was first occupied, the vicinity around it contained more open grassland, fewer juniper trees, and far more grass than today. During the years that the site was occupied, the number of junipers remained low, some undoubtedly being cut for use in construction and as fuel. At the same time, the proportion of pollen from the weedy perennials that invade disturbed land around human settlements (e.g., cheno-ams) increased. Toward the end of Shoofly's occupation, the proportion of juniper pollen increased significantly, indicating a change in the surrounding area toward a denser woodland.

Pollen samples analyzed from several small sites in neighboring Star Valley provided comparative information for what was already learned from Shoofly Village (Gregory 1991a). Corroborating the macrobotanical evidence from the same sites in Star Valley, the pollen indicates that corn was present at almost every large and small site investigated. The discovery of corn as the major economic plant resource at sites of all sizes underscores its ubiquity in the subsistence pursuits of virtually all groups during the late prehistoric period. Pollen from cheno-am was also found associated with many of the sites, as would be expected, but its economic importance may have been more limited than it was at Shoofly. Gregory (1991a) suggests that only at one of the small upland zone sites, Site 639, was there sufficient cheno-am pollen to conclude that is was used prehistorically. Another important discovery from sites in the upland zones was the presence of oak pollen, especially the abundance of oak pollen found in a sample taken from a roasting pit at Site 639, which indicated both its presence in the local forest and its use as a fuel.

The pollen samples from Site 620, the largest site investigated in the Star Valley area, also revealed a pattern of changing juniper cover similar to that at Shoofly. The evidence indicates that during the occupation of the site, junipers were relatively scarce and cheno-ams and grasses were relatively abundant. As the site was being abandoned, the proportion of junipers increased dramatically, reaching higher pollen densities than those indicated by modern samples from the site. Then, sometime between abandonment and the present time, the proportion of junipers decreased once again, perhaps as a result of human use or climatic change in the area.

Animal Resources

Fortunately for an understanding of the prehistoric diet of the people in this region, faunal remains were relatively common at Shoofly Village and at other sites in the region. The basic pattern that emerges from this evidence is that the people of the Tonto Rim hunted deer and rabbits as their primary source of meat. This is true at many sites in the Southwest. Interestingly, we recovered no convincing evidence of domestic turkeys or dogs. For a listing of the various animal species found in the deposits of Shoofly Village and other Payson area sites see Appendix 4.

One important observation from Shoofly Village and the hamlet settlements we excavated was that deer bones were more common than rabbit bones (Eshbaugh 1988:129). This contrasts with the findings from many other Arizona sites where the opposite pattern is present. What makes our pattern even more significant is the obvious fact that the amount of meat available from a deer is many times larger than that from an individual rabbit, multiplying the resulting effect on the diet. Another trend we found was that small sites generally had very few animal bones, and when they did have them, there were only rabbit bones and no deer remains present. If this trend reflects a true prehistoric pattern rather than a sampling problem, it documents the presence of simple, opportunistic hunting at small sites, if any hunting took place at all. This undermines a common assumption that these small camps frequently served as specialized hunting stations.

One settlement where the proportion of rabbits was higher than deer was Scorpion Rock Ruin, specifically in its pithouse deposits. We have attributed the pithouse buildings to an early Hohokam-related occupation, which might help explain the difference in meat procurement practices compared with the majority of other sites in the region. Site 650, which does not have any pithouse features but does have considerable ceramic evidence of Hohokam connections, also exhibits a relatively large number of rabbit remains, although it is still somewhat less than deer.

The importance of deer to the prehistoric people of this region is highlighted by the surprising discovery of 55 deer mandibles in room 5 at Deer Jaw Ruin hamlet (Hohmann and Atwell 1988). The excavators have interpreted this not as evidence of a ceremonial use for the room but rather as a possible "trophy" or record-keeping cache in an otherwise normal habitation room. While there were no other deer crania fragments in the room, there were 11 other deer bones, 18 cottontail rabbit bones, 9 jackrabbit bones, and 1 canvas-back duck bone. The excavators have suggested that this room housed a family or task group that specialized in hunting and distributed meat to others in the hamlet and, perhaps, to the neighboring primary village of Risser Ranch.

Although much less bulky and fewer in number than deer, rabbits provided a key element in the meat consumption of the people of this region. It is likely that rabbits could be hunted close to a base camp or village. They could be caught in traps that were set ahead of time and then collected at any time later. Thus, hunting rabbits would not conflict with the pursuit of other activities. We also expect that rabbits would have been available year-round and in sufficient numbers so that they were, in effect, always available. This would make them a reliable source of meat during difficult periods or when people were occupied with other tasks and could not mount an organized deer hunt. The faunal collections from most sites contained a greater number of cottontail rabbits than jackrabbits. This indicates that the environment near settlements, or at least where rabbits were procured, was dominated by brush and tree cover, which is favored by cottontails, rather than by an open grassland habitat, which is favored by jackrabbits.

Not surprisingly, all rabbit body parts were represented in the collections, indicating that the entire carcass was brought back to the site. Traces of burning on the bones suggests that the animals were roasted over a fire and that the hind legs were separated from the body before roasting and consumption. More surprising, however, was the discovery that in virtually all of the settlements where they were present, deer bones represented all parts of the body, indicating that the entire carcass of this large species was brought back to the settlement. This is important because, at some contemporaneous settlements in the Hohokam periphery north of Phoenix, some of the primary meat-bearing bones were underrepresented, leaving open the possibility that meat was being sent from these sites to larger communities in the Salt-Gila River valley (Eshbaugh 1988). In contrast to rabbit bones, deer bones were usually burned all over, indicating that after they were roasted and the meat was consumed the bones were thrown into the fire.

Our evidence indicates that most of the animal resources used by the prehistoric inhabitants of the Payson region could have been procured within a short distance of their settlement, probably 5 km or less (Fig. 9.1). In addition to those species already discussed, our evidence reveals that these people also hunted elk, bear, bighorn, coyote, antelope jackrabbit, and smaller animals, such as mud turtle and squirrel (Eshbaugh 1988). For the most part these animals could be found near the Payson settlements, but the normal range for elk and Abert's squirrel would have been 20 km to the north, above the Mogollon Rim, and for antelope jackrabbits it would have been twice that distance to the south in the lower elevations. It is likely that elk and antelope jackrabbits were procured on long-distance forays mounted specifically for hunting or some other activity.

A modest number of bird bones was found at Shoofly and other sites. These included bones from hawks, ravens, flickers, and a single bone each from a mallard and a crane. Given that only 35 bird bones were found in the Shoofly Village collection of over 4,000 bones (and similar proportions from the other investigations), it appears that birds were only a minor source of meat for the people of this region. Eshbaugh has hypothesized that, because wing bones are overrepresented, hawks and other birds may have been taken primarily for the ceremonial use of their plumage, rather than as a source of meat.

Osteological Evidence on Diet

It is possible to learn some very important things about the diet and living conditions of prehistoric people from a careful study of their skeletal remains. People were not buried at the majority of sites in the Payson area. We expect that this was due to the short duration of occupation at many small household communities. The number of people who would have died while residing at a short-term settlement would be relatively small. It is possible, as well, that for some groups it

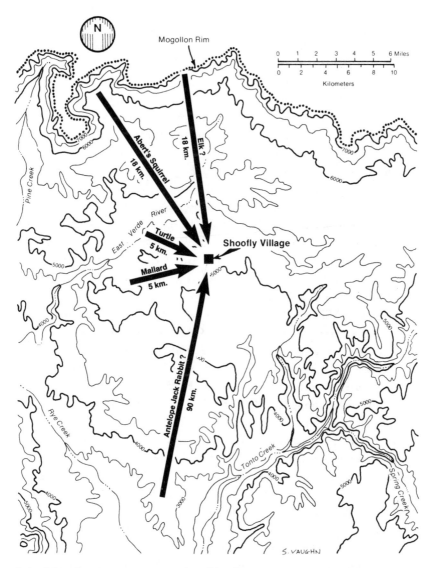

9.1   Map showing procurement localities for common animal resources
consumed by the people of Shoofly Village. (Adapted from Eshbaugh 1988.)

was customary to inter the dead at what might have been an ancestral village community, rather than at a temporary settlement. Not surprisingly, almost all of the human burials encountered were at Shoofly Village, while only a few individuals were recovered from hamlets like Site 620 and Deer Jaw Ruin, and even fewer individuals were uncovered at small household sites. Burials included individuals of various ages, ranging from infancy to 50 years old.

The overall impression provided by the skeletal material is that the people of the Tonto Rim were of average stature and were reasonably healthy for a prehistoric population (Atwell and Menkhus 1991; Ivanhoe 1985; Morris 1990). Despite this positive bill of health, it should be recognized that, in general, the people of the Southwest lived under difficult conditions. Almost all of the skeletons recovered by our project showed signs of dental enamel hypoplasia, reflecting episodes of calcium deficiency in their diets. Bones from over half of the population revealed evidence of porotic hyperostosis and/or cribra orbitalia, once again indicating an inadequate diet. Two individuals appear to have had osteoarthritis, several had trauma fractures, and a few had a variety of irregularly fused bones.

At Shoofly Village, almost all of the skeletons were found in one of two areas that we might call cemeteries. One cemetery was located in the general area we refer to as the south plaza and may have predated the south roomblock. This is where the majority of burials were located, and they probably derive from the first two phases of Shoofly's occupation. The skeletons were extended and lying on their backs, usually with their heads facing east or southeast. In some cases, one or two simple vessels were associated with the body and a pile of rocks were placed over the grave. The second cemetery was located outside the compound wall to the north. It is possible that once the south roomblock was built the cemetery in the plaza area was no longer suitable, and other locations were substituted. A distinctive burial in the northern cemetery contained two mature individuals who appear to have been laid out together with a completely intact bowl and a deer long bone awl among their grave goods.

Careful interment also seems to have been the rule at Site 620, while at other sites it appears that the burials were disturbed by later activity in the area because only small fragments have been recovered. It should be noted that, while inhumations seem to have been the preferred

burial pattern at most Payson settlements, there is evidence that crema-
tion was practiced at two of the sites with Hohokam-like material (early
Scorpion Rock and Site 491).

Although much of the recovered material is fragmentary, there were
several instances where it was clear that the individuals had deformed
skulls. This trait has commonly been found among sedentary agricultural populations in the prehistoric Southwest and is often attributed
to the use of a hard-backed cradle board for infants. The Shoofly
remains exhibit a pronounced flattening of the back of the skull vault
around the lambda, possibly enhanced by binding the skull to the
cradle board around the forehead. The total effect of this practice is to
raise the back crown of the head, providing a distinctly taller appearance to the individual. Although we have no specific evidence to cor-
roborate this suggestion, it is possible that the deformation was deliberate and encouraged among individuals, possibly being perceived as
beautiful or as a sign of group identity.

In sum, it is clear from the archaeological evidence that the people of
the Tonto Rim effectively pursued a variety of local food sources. They
were effective maize farmers and their meat came largely from hunting
deer. Beyond these two major food sources a wide variety of resources
were utilized, probably in response to a poor harvest or lack of game.
Some of these, such as rabbits and the intensely harvested wild plants
cheno-am and purslane, were used so regularly that they, too, must
have become essential to the diet. Beyond these, a wide variety of plants
and animals were consumed on a far more infrequent, opportunistic
basis. What this reflects are groups of sophisticated farmers and hunters
who primarily specialized in the most productive food sources but
maintained a familiarity and modest reliance on a much wider selection
of food sources. As in other pursuits, this reveals the people of the
region to be concerned with flexibility in their lifestyle even while
becoming relatively specialized.

10 □ □ *The Past Revisited*
□

When trying to synthesize our knowledge of the past and draw out its broader implications, the archaeologist relies on a variety of sources. Primary among them are the material remains left behind by the actual people who are of interest to us: their architecture, artifacts, and subsistence remains. In earlier chapters we have reviewed this information as it was brought to light by our expedition and by the work of other researchers. We have also looked at the general potential for settlement in the region by evaluating its environmental characteristics and its use during historic times. This approach derives from our reliance on the principle of uniformitarianism, which states that the processes of the past can be best understood in terms of the on-going processes of the present.

The uniformitarian principle pervades archaeological thinking, especially in the American Southwest where environmental extremes constrain lifestyles and where early accounts of Native Americans in the region provide a living model of what might have existed in the more distant past. As exciting and stimulating as these potential analogies have been to archaeologists for the past century, we must be careful not to restrict ourselves to reconstructing the past only in the image of what we have seen in the present. In this final chapter, I attempt to use the insights gained from our own work and from other sources to speculate on a few issues that are not easily addressed by analogies from the present. The first section deals with climatic change and its potential ramifications for human settlement in the Payson area. The second section reviews the settlement types defined in this volume and examines their broader implications. The third part discusses how the absence of decorated ceramics in the region may reflect a prehistoric social order that is still poorly understood. Finally, we end with the enduring archaeological question: Where did they go? To suggest an answer, we draw on several lines of evidence to flesh out what we believe is an important episode in Southwestern prehistory.

Past to Present Climatic Continuum

Most experts would agree that the topography, climate, and natural biotic communities of the Payson-Star Valley region have remained relatively constant over the past millennium. Our own archaeological evidence indicates that, in general, the same plants and animals that are available today were available during the prehistoric occupation of Shoofly Village, except for some changes caused by a century of cattle grazing and the introduction of modern plants. The juniper was the most common tree in the prehistoric record, as it is today. The main difference is that the proportion of junipers was probably higher in the past. According to pollen evidence collected by Gregory (1989), the density of junipers may have increased further during the occupation of Shoofly, perhaps reaching a peak. Our excavations recovered numerous samples of carbonized wood, yet there was no ponderosa pine and less than 10 percent of the pieces recovered at Shoofly were pinyon pine. This accurately reflects the current tree cover in the immediate vicinity of Shoofly Village, although both ponderosa and pinyon pine trees are more plentiful a short distance away. Given that both would have served as desirable building material for spanning the large rooms found at Shoofly, their absence indicates that the occupants were unwilling to haul the wood or, more likely, that these trees were virtually absent from the immediate area during the site's occupation.

Another important change in the local vegetation is that, before the introduction of cattle grazing, grasses and other herbaceous plants would have been more abundant. Grass seeds were found among the macrobotanical samples from the excavations, and grass pollen was especially common in the early phases of occupation. I expect that the presence of more grasses in the area would have facilitated soil development and inhibited erosion so that the local soils were somewhat deeper in prehistoric times than they are now. Overall, this modest difference would have made the immediate vicinity of Shoofly and many other localities in the region more hospitable to agriculture 1,000 years ago than they are today.

Another line of evidence that can be used to evaluate past climates is derived from studying the annual tree rings of wood associated with the prehistoric occupation of archaeological sites. Unfortunately, Shoofly Village and the other sites in this region have failed to yield wood samples that are amenable to tree-ring analysis. The Laboratory of Climatology at the University of Arizona, however, has collected tree ring information from throughout central Arizona and has attempted to reconstruct the rainfall patterns in the Upper Verde and Salt River drainages (Nials, Gregory, and Graybill 1989). Their model is based on studies of tree samples from historic times, which show that the width of an annual tree ring correlates well with the amount of rainfall recorded that year in the immediate area.

The most interesting aspect of the study involves the year-to-year variability of rainfall. This would have been particularly important for agriculturalists who relied on rain to water their crops. Three time periods are of particular interest to us here: A.D. 900–1051, A.D. 1052–1196, and A.D. 1197–1355. During the first period there was relatively consistent rainfall from year to year, especially after A.D. 980. During the second period, there were years of extreme rainfall about once every 20 years: half of them were high and the other half were low rainfall years. Most likely, only those years of low rainfall would have presented a serious problem to prehistoric farmers. During the last period the frequency doubled to one extreme year each decade. Moreover, the extremes became much greater, especially during dry years. From A.D. 1210 to A.D. 1310 there were ten years of extremely low rainfall and, we can assume, widespread crop failures.

The tree-ring information portrays a climate that was quite condu-
cive to rainfall agriculture, especially from A.D. 980 to about A.D. 1140.
From A.D. 1140 on, the frequency and magnitude of drought years
increased, making it more and more difficult to maintain an agrarian
way of life dependent on rainfall alone. The occasional bad year in the
larger, more organized settlements might have been mitigated by the
use of stored surpluses but, given the frequent failures in the thirteenth
century, even this might have been inadequate.

Although direct evidence is still incomplete, I hypothesize that some
of the farmers left their land in the Payson area and moved to farmland
where surface-water irrigation could supplement what they received in
rainfall, substantially increasing the probability of having successful
crops. By understanding that extremes in precipitation are also haz-
ardous to irrigation farmers, the most successful farmers during this era
would most likely be those who relied on several water sources for their
crops. I would argue that just this type of situation might have existed
in the Tonto Basin, where rainfall was supplemented with both runoff
irrigation and river irrigation. It is at about this time, A.D. 1200, that
the population of the Tonto Basin mushroomed and that of the Payson
region began a steady decline. We will return to this theme in the final
section of this chapter.

The Prehistoric Settlement System Revisited

What are the essential elements of the prehistoric community types that
we have defined for the Payson area, and in what ways has our understanding of Southwestern prehistory been expanded by studying them?
The household community, hamlet, and agricultural village each had
its own history of success in the Payson region and, possibly, beyond.
Without confining myself to a rigid documentation of each idea, I
would like to discuss in a more speculative manner whether these settlements originated in another region, how they operated together, and
what happened to them in the thirteenth and fourteenth centuries when
the Payson-Star Valley area was gradually abandoned.

The household community is the smallest and most common of the
Payson settlement types. These settlements comprised small self-suffi-

cient groups of individuals drawn together by family ties or by devotion to a task group that relied on extensive maize agriculture practiced in the scattered plots of cultivatable soil that characterize much of the Payson region. I envision the group of people at these two- to six-room sites as mobile and largely autonomous. Without large quantities of material goods and living in modestly constructed houses, they could inhabit a particular locality for as short a time as a single agricultural season and then move on if the soil became depleted or proved inadequate to support their farming activities. The small size of the cultivatable plots throughout the upland zone and in much of the creek zone surrounding Payson would favor communities small enough to survive on the yield of a few hectares of maize, supplemented by hunting and modest gathering of wild plant foods. My hypothesis that these were relatively autonomous units rests on several lines of evidence. First, all household community sites that we have examined closely had evidence of maize consumption and contained a diversity of artifacts reflecting a wide range of activities. Second, the ceramics at these small sites often showed evidence of having been produced at more than one or even several larger sites, indicating the absence of a strong relationship with a single large settlement. Third, their small size and high mobility would allow members of household communities to "fit in among the cracks" of the settlement system without upsetting established relationships among larger communities. In fact, some of these people probably moved into and out of larger hamlets and villages as the need for resources and other goods dictated.

Although they can succeed economically, small family-size communities would have had to draw together in some arrangement to find mates and to celebrate events with ceremonial activities. This may have taken the form of alliances or ceremonial rounds, similar to those known from ethnographic studies. Cooperation among small co-equal communities would have operated best in regions where they were not affected by the presence of a group with a strong centralized organization demanding their allegiance. The autonomous pattern would flourish in regions where centralized authority failed to develop or in regions that were beyond the control of those authorities. For most of its history, Payson appears to have fit that description.

Because of their numbers, household communities could be considered the characteristic Payson settlement type. It should be recognized, however, that their large number is offset by their short-term use and by the small number of people who inhabited each. The impression from archaeological surveys is that, up to A.D. 1100, there were few small sites, but they were the only form of occupation in the region. Starting at about A.D. 1100, the number of small sites increased dramatically. Up to this time, small sites seem to have consisted of a diversity of types, but after A.D. 1100 they appear to be of a single, consistent type. It should be remembered, however, that the establishment of hamlets and villages during this same period reflected an even larger population increase, housing the majority of the region's inhabitants. Although the data are quite limited, it is my impression that as the population of the region diminished during the thirteenth century household communities were abandoned as fast as the larger sites and perhaps disappeared first, being outlived by a few hamlets (e.g., Site 620 and Scorpion Rock Ruin) and village centers (e.g., Risser Ranch). This would indicate that whatever forces gave rise to the original, low-density settlement of the region before A.D. 1000 were the same forces that were upset by the end of the thirteenth century when the Payson region was left with virtually no permanent residents.

As speculative as it is to estimate population distribution among the different site types, it is even more difficult to specify the social and economic relationships among those settlements. During the height of occupation in the region (ca. A.D. 1100–1250), it is possible that an integrated settlement system with strong interdependence between various site types existed. One scenario is that household communities served as seasonal habitations or work localities to which small groups from larger sites would come to tend fields, hunt animals, or collect ripening plants or special resources. These groups would then return to the larger settlement for part of the year or, at least, for special ceremonial periods.

An alternative view is that small household sites with architecture operated as independent communities, much like the small settlements that existed before the growth of the centers. This scenario depicts a less centralized settlement system of dispersed groups, each more or less self-sufficient, that might have come together on rare occasions to secure mates from groups outside their immediate family. It should be recognized that, for this system to exist, there would have had to be some form of shared beliefs or alliances that would allow many semi-independent groups to coexist in the same region. Although I favor this interpretation, I readily acknowledge that the situation was dynamic and probably changed during the period of occupation as economic strategies evolved and new forces arose from outside the region.

In my opinion, the type of communities that we have referred to as hamlets have a significance that goes beyond the Payson region, since they occur in other regions and at other time periods. As they have been found in the Payson region, these settlements had from six to forty rooms, but those with a large number of rooms probably represent several phases of occupation. I would argue that the hamlets in the Payson region had in use at any one point in time between six and twelve rooms, usually toward the lower end of that range. This size would represent a social unit that may not have an exact ethnographic analog but might have comprised a group of closely related families similar to a clan. Its organization may have been structured along kinship lines, without major distinctions in rank and status. Containing anywhere from 20 to as many as 100 individuals, the hamlets could have been largely self-sufficient in economic activities, although I believe they had stronger ties to a particular primary village than the household communities did. It would have been possible to assemble enough people from a hamlet for organized hunting forays or medium-distance procurement expeditions. They would also have provided adequate labor for modest agricultural construction projects, such as check dams and small-scale irrigation systems. Although these communities usually would have been permanent, year-round settlements, it is possible that some of the larger ones split up into smaller hamlets during difficult times.

I also expect that some form of cooperation existed among the various hamlets of a region. Without good evidence on the issue, I would suggest that in most situations hamlets would have maintained a reciprocal exchange relationship between each other involving at least some goods. However, in some circumstances, including the twelfth century in the Payson region, these inter-hamlet relationships may have become hierarchical, with one or more hamlets (or clans) becoming strongly associated with a particular primary village. As outlined in Chapter 8, our best evidence for this comes from the undecorated ceramics. The mineralogical composition of pottery found at several hamlets indicates that it was made at certain primary villages. In each case, the hamlet was geographically close to the primary village, further supporting the inference that hamlets relied on specific villages for most of their ceramics. This interdependence and trade between hamlets and villages may have been a major factor in the growth of larger sites in the Payson-Star Valley area and elsewhere.

Communities of the size that I have defined as hamlets are found throughout the early sedentary village societies of the Southwest, and they may have had a similar social organization. As many of them coalesced into larger population centers, they appear to have maintained their own identity. This autonomy may have reflected something as simple as individual family groups or more substantial differences that we might characterize as ethnic or, at least, as people derived from a distinct cultural tradition. I see the courtyard compounds of the Hohokam (Rice 1984) as an excellent example of the continuation of this community form within a larger aggregation. The "unit" pueblos (Lekson 1991) of the Mogollon, and possibly even of the Anasazi, may represent a similar phenomenon— maintaining autonomy in some situations but being governed by the larger, seemingly homogenous communities in other situations.

Hamlets appear to have continued to exist in the Payson area as long as the larger villages and smaller household communities did. Although the disappearance of large agricultural villages in the Payson area could be interpreted as reflecting a breakdown of the social organization, the concurrent disappearance of hamlets, which represent a potential source of social groups for new aggregated villages, unambiguously signals the end of large settlements in this region.

Of the large agricultural villages of the Payson region, only Shoofly Village has been extensively studied; therefore, the full range of variability among villages has not yet been revealed. As was described in Chapter 5, Shoofly Village appears to have grown by the addition of coherent units and by the expansion of the units themselves. Architecturally, the units resemble hamlets, opening the possibility that before they established themselves at Shoofly Village the people of each unit may have comprised a separate, autonomous hamlet community. It is also possible that each unit maintained some of its autonomy, even after becoming part of the larger community at Shoofly Village.

My current reconstruction of the organizational history of Shoofly Village is that it was established as a hamlet in a favorable setting and attracted other families and, perhaps, other hamlet populations. Around the beginning of the twelfth century a different type of hamlet community joined Shoofly Village and this group built the central part of the core roomblock. This transformed what had been a loose association of three or four hamlets at one location into a more integrated settlement. The village continued to grow through the addition of at least two more hamlets and the filling in of more rooms to accommodate either internal population growth or the immigration of household communities. Although I believe the clan that occupied the core roomblock at Shoofly Village was probably more highly ranked and may have exerted control over other component units in the village, I see no reason to suggest that the use of force was a factor in the growth of Shoofly Village. Rather, I envision a situation in which other large agricultural villages were being established in the Payson region and beyond, leading the people of Shoofly to emulate in their own settlement what was becoming a viable community form.

Although it is difficult to be sure without more research, the layout of rooms at other Payson-area villages, inferred from surface reconnaissance, suggests that they too may have had pueblo-like roomblocks at their center. Mayfield Canyon, Risser Ranch, and Round Valley all appear to have additional rooms dispersed around their core roomblocks, but from surface indications they do not resemble a hamlet form nor do all of them include the obviously subrectangular rooms present at Shoofly. In these cases, the village may have grown around a large core population by internal growth or immigration of household communities or individuals from hamlets, rather than by the annexation of entire hamlet groups, as we have hypothesized for Shoofly Village.

Interestingly, while Mayfield Canyon and Risser Ranch villages were occupied, hamlets continued to exist in their immediate vicinities. Contrary to this pattern, no hamlets have been discovered in the immediate vicinity of Shoofly Village. The closest hamlet we know of is Site 04-59, which is located 2 km to the south below the rim of Houston Mesa. Incomplete as it is, both the site layout and site location information indicate that Shoofly Village was more of an aggregation of distinct hamlet units that maintained some autonomy internally and isolation externally than were the other large agricultural villages in the region.

Decorated Ceramics and the Social Order

One of the nagging questions facing archaeologists who have worked in the Payson region and in other areas of central Arizona is why the people of Shoofly Village and of the Payson region in general produced no decorated ceramics at all. Contemporaneous societies only 50 or 100 km away produced quantities of decorated ceramics, and the Payson-area people were equally proficient in many technologies. If ornamentation had no particular meaning in society, then its absence could be just an accident in the way traditional pottery making evolved. I think it is unlikely that this is a sufficient explanation for the complete absence of painted ceramics in the Payson-Star Valley area.

Rather, I suggest that painted decoration on ceramics, as well as other forms of decoration, served a function within prehistoric society, as it does today. The significance varied, but it may have included such purposes as identifying membership in a social group or defining the use of certain artifacts. The key question then is whether the people of Shoofly and of other areas of central Arizona satisfied these requirements by using other media, such as body painting or the ornamentation of perishable materials such as wood, or whether the need for this type of expression was relatively low among them. I suspect that the truth is some combination of the two.

It is not easy to know what other materials might have been decorated, but baskets, textiles, wood, leather, and even the human body are all possibilities. To date, remains of these materials are almost completely absent from the archaeological record in the Payson area due to the lack of preservation. If we had the artifacts, we would probably find some that were decorated, but I believe the second possibility—altered needs within the society—is the more important one to explore.

Numerous anthropologists and art historians have discussed the range of functions that decorative behavior can play in society (Davis

1990; Longacre 1970; S. Plog 1980; Wobst 1977). One of the most general and pervasive explanation is that it serves to regulate and communicate social order. This is particularly true when other integrating mechanisms, such as written laws, are absent (Redman 1978). My argument is that during certain periods some societies developed the need for greater information flow and regulation than could be achieved by the normal channels of kinship, language, and dress. Situations that may lead to these increased needs are a growing population size and an increasing settlement density. For example, during A.D. 1000–1250 the Anasazi seemed to have experienced general population growth as well as very large population aggregations. The abundance of Anasazi decorated ceramics, which are characterized by a structured layout and repetitive designs, were one means of communicating detailed information and thus helped to mediate the increasing social complexity that accompanied population growth. In the absence of major breakthroughs in social control, such as new religious doctrine, social stratification, writing, or organized militarism, decorated ceramics may have been one of several important media for communicating the appropriate social and economic order. At Anasazi sites, decorated vessels often account for 30 to 50 percent of the assemblage, with much of the remainder being composed of corrugated vessels, which many archaeologists consider to be decorated as well.

In contrast, most ceramic assemblages of the Hohokam and their possible cousins, the Salado, appear to have less than 10 percent decorated vessels, and their decorative schemes appear to be less structured and repetitive than those of the Anasazi. I would argue that the Hohokam maintained the importance of smaller social units and less tightly aggregated settlements. While decorated ceramics probably played an integrative role, they may have been used only for certain activities or their access may have been restricted to prescribed members of the society. Moreover, I suspect that the Hohokam and Salado had others means of social control and information flow, which were not part of Anasazi culture. Although we do not yet fully understand their function, such features as ball courts and platform mounds at Hohokam and Salado sites may reflect the existence of some new forms of social integration or ordering (Wilcox and Sternberg 1983).

As I suggested in the introduction to this book, the culture of the people of the Payson-Star Valley area may have developed along a much different course than that of the Anasazi or Hohokam. The "classic" manifestations of the Anasazi and Hohokam are large population aggregations, massive architecture, and abundant decorative objects. I propose that decorative behavior, just like the repetitive nature of the architecture in their settlements, is a means of adjusting to and controlling the social order in these large communities. The fact that decorated ceramics and orderly building plans also occur in peripheral Anasazi areas can be attributed to an ethnic or social tradition that was defined in the centers but was carried on in the periphery more to reaffirm membership than to satisfy any of the needs that gave rise to the original behavior in the core areas.

But what of the people of Shoofly Village, the Payson area, and much of the vast basin and range complex of central Arizona? As we discussed earlier, the temperate climate, the diverse topography, and the availability of natural resources minimized the need for major population aggregations and close control of production and population, which were required—temporarily at least—on both the higher Colorado Plateau and the lower Arizona desert lands. The size of social units and even of aggregated settlements in central Arizona remained small-scale. At least in the case of Shoofly Village where the actual number of inhabitants may have approached that of an Anasazi central settlement, the constituent social units appear to have maintained more autonomy than we hypothesize for their grander neighbors.

Thus, there was no pressing need for social identity or social control beyond the minimal social units at Shoofly and probably at many other Payson-area communities. Ceramics seemed to have functioned in a more restricted utilitarian fashion, such as food preparation, serving, and storage without broader social significance. Interestingly, among many of the decorated pottery types of the Southwest, bowl forms are more common than jar forms. Because they are used primarily for food serving and final preparation, bowls are more likely to be an important media for communicating to people outside the immediate family than are jars, which are used primarily for storage. In the Payson area, it is clear that jars are more common and that the diversity of jars is greater than that of bowls. Once again, the evidence from the people of Payson reveals a diminished focus on producing vessel forms that would be involved in stylistic communication and, instead, a concentration on highly adaptable utilitarian forms.

What Happened in Prehistory

The implication that I have drawn from the absence of decorated ceramics is that the basic organizational structure of the people of the Payson region—and perhaps of a much broader area of the Southwest—was far looser and less formal than that of the Anasazi. Household communities fit in around the edges, locating themselves away from larger settlements and maintaining only minimal communication with them. Hamlets were small enough that residents could regulate their own community along informal kinship lines, and everyone understood their role and rank without a need for extensive use of stylistic symbols. At least in the Payson area, hamlets were established in a dispersed pattern across the landscape, similar to household units, in order to take advantage of small, widely separated patches of suitable agricultural land.

It is the absence of decorated ceramics at the larger agricultural villages in the Payson-Star Valley area, and in other central Arizona regions, that is more difficult to understand. Part of the answer may be that the modest size and dispersed distribution of settlements failed to engender competition among neighbors for food and other resources in the surrounding countryside. But it is more than that. I believe that by maintaining the semiautonomy of the constituent hamlets the organizational structure of the entire village remained simple, and regulation could be accomplished with a minimal use of abstract symbols. In addition, the people of Payson appear to have been largely self-sufficient with little reliance on long-distance trade contacts. Participation in commerce with other regions would be another potential reason to utilize widely "understood" traditional symbols on decorated pottery, but our evidence indicates that this was not a part of life in prehistoric Payson.

What is remarkable about the social organization in the Payson region during the twelfth and thirteenth centuries is that, in fact, it operated successfully without some of the organizational trappings we see in other regions at this time. Moreover, during this interval, there were quite a few people living in the general area. I believe that the system attained its greatest population size in the years around A.D. 1200 when all of the larger agricultural villages and probably three-fourths of the hamlets were occupied. I would estimate that, taken together, these villages and hamlets would have been inhabited by 1,000 to 1,500 people. The household communities were probably occupied more briefly; hence, at any one time, only a fraction of the known household communities would have been inhabited. This more mobile population probably fluctuated greatly, with people moving in and out of the region or to and from larger settlements, but a reasonable estimate for any one time would be about 500 individuals. This brings the maximum population for the region at its zenith to an estimated 2,000 people—small by modern standards but quite impressive in terms of the low population densities of the prehistoric Southwest.

Our own excavations and archaeological surveys, as well as those by others, indicate that by A.D. 1300, and probably a bit earlier, the Payson region had been depopulated. The population probably began to decline soon after A.D. 1200, and by A.D. 1250 Shoofly Village and several of the outlying hamlets were very likely already abandoned. We believe that throughout the thirteenth century settlements were slowly abandoned without the formation of new communities. Based largely on the presence of datable pottery from Risser Ranch, Scorpion Rock Ruin, and Site 620, we believe that some of the sites in the creek zone south of Shoofly Village continued to be inhabited until the end of the thirteenth century. In fact, what may have occurred during the second half of the thirteenth century is a contraction of the population into the larger valleys where the modern towns of Payson and Star Valley are located.

What might have caused this contraction or shift? One possibility is the movement of other people into the country to the north, above the Mogollon Rim. Evidence from other projects indicates that population movements and site aggregation were, in fact, taking place at this time on the Colorado Plateau. An alternative possibility is related to local agricultural production and climatic cycles. Our excavations have shown that, from the smallest to the largest settlements we have examined, the Payson-Star Valley people relied on maize agriculture. Their artifact inventory includes a preponderance of plant processing tools and storage vessels. They were clearly agriculturalists who had selected a region with reasonable agricultural potential and had established themselves there during a period of favorable climatic conditions. The Payson-Star Valley region, however, also has a relatively poor and localized soil development that would have deteriorated after a relatively short period of agricultural use. The vicinity around Shoofly would be particularly vulnerable; the open territory surrounding the settlement would easily be denuded of necessary soil for agriculture, and nearby arroyos would not offer sufficient arable land to support agriculture watered by runoff.

The abandonment of Shoofly and of most hamlets and small household sites in the region may be viewed as part of the thirteenth-century movement to the south and the development of new population centers that relied more heavily on irrigation agriculture. The people may have initially moved into neighboring settlements in the Payson region, such as Risser Ranch. By the end of the century, however, the majority of them had migrated south and west, most likely joining the growing settlements in the Tonto Basin and Verde River Valley. The question then becomes whether their movement out of the Payson region was motivated by a need to escape from settlers from the north, a search for new agricultural land, or an attraction to the new social and political forms developing in the Tonto Basin and elsewhere.

The fourteenth century across much of the Southwestern highlands and deserts is characterized by large aggregated communities. Although a debate on the subject continues, it is likely that many, or even all, of these settlements were organized along hierarchical lines with various centralizing institutions (see Upham, Lightfoot, and Jewett 1989). We also know from archaeological evidence that long-distance trade in polychrome ceramics and other goods linked many of these settlements together, and that these goods may have provided some of the basis for their ceremonial and organizational structure.

It is also possible that many of the people of the Payson region ultimately went north to live in large settlements, such as those on Anderson Mesa (Upham 1982); east to join such communities as Grasshopper pueblo or Point of Pines; or west to the Verde River Valley.

Several lines of evidence, however, indicate that a significant portion of the Payson people moved south into the Tonto Basin. The geography would favor a movement to Tonto Basin, both because it is easy to reach and because it is the closest river valley that could support large numbers of irrigation agriculturalists.

The most convincing evidence comes from similarities in the ceramic inventories of the Payson and Tonto Basin people. The basic approach to the manufacture of undecorated ceramics is similar in the two regions, with Tonto-Verde brownwares from both areas nearly indistinguishable. In both regions pottery was constructed using a paddle and anvil technique; by contrast, the analogous plainware made at communities located above the Mogollon Rim was formed predominantly by a coil and scrape technique.

Equally convincing are several distinctive architectural features. The first is the unusually large room size that we have found at sites in the Payson area and are now beginning to find in the Tonto Basin as well. Perhaps the most suggestive evidence is the spatial layout of certain settlements in the Tonto Basin that resemble that of the hamlets in the Payson area. These are what Rice calls individual compound communities (1990). Even more intriguing is the presence of easily distinguishable components that resemble hamlets at several large Tonto Basin sites. These are conceptually similar to those at Shoofly Village, but they are 100 years later and their community size and overall population density is considerably higher (Redman, Rice, and Pedrick 1992). Archaeological fieldwork is still continuing, but the initial picture of several roomblocks that were originally built separately from one another on the platform mound, as well as in the community of small settlements surrounding the Schoolhouse Point Platform Mound, is very suggestive of Shoofly Village and other Payson villages, but on a larger scale (Fig. 10.1).

If our views accurately reflect what happened in prehistory, they point to several issues that only now are beginning to receive adequate discussion in the archaeological literature. The first issue involves the nature of a functioning prehistoric community and how that relates to an archaeologically discovered settlement system. Our response to this question has been the proposal of three basic settlement types for the Payson region. Beyond the types themselves, there are two innovations

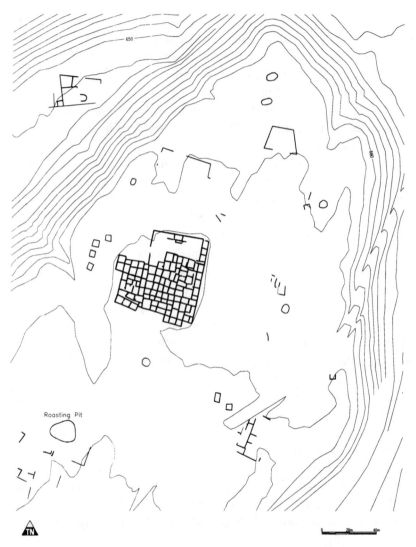

Roasting Pit

10.1   Map of Schoolhouse Point Platform Mound Complex in the Tonto
Basin.

in our thinking: first, we have suggested that the smallest communities
contained single households that were largely self-sufficient from their
larger neighbors; and second, we have proposed that the largest settlements were fragile aggregations of smaller hamlets that retained some

degree of autonomy within what are defined archaeologically as single communities. The new perspective advocated here is the pervasive and enduring autonomy of small-scale social units among the prehistoric people of Payson, and probably across a much larger area of the Southwest.

The second issue raised by the Payson settlement pattern was the appearance of a rapid increase and an equally rapid decline in the population of the region. Starting around A.D. 800, the regional population may have numbered less than 100 permanent residents; by A.D. 1200, it had increased to as many as 2,000 inhabitants; 100 years later, it had dropped back to less than 100. This rapid change makes us reconsider notions of mobility as they are currently understood. Mobility among hunters and gatherers and early agriculturalists is widely recognized, but the important point here is that the Payson-area people were firmly established agriculturalists, down to the smallest settlement. The conclusion one can draw from this is that the key constraint imposed on prehistoric groups by the environment in much of the Southwest was not so much the limitation on localities where agriculture can be practiced, as the limitation on the length of time agriculture can be practiced in those locations. Except for the reliable, riverine irrigation settings, the soils of the Southwest seem to be able to sustain agricultural groups for only one or, at the most, two centuries. At least this seems to be the picture that emerges from the Payson region, and once again we believe that it may explain population movements out of many other regions as well.

The important point I want to derive from this is that mobility must be seen as a basic process of Southwestern existence. Recent theorists (e.g., Upham 1982) often rely on alliance formation and trade in basic goods to explain how the uneven productivity of various regions was balanced or offset. We must now add to those theories the movement of people—perhaps more frequently than the movement of foodstuffs—to balance these temporal and geographic insufficiencies.

The third issue emerging from the Payson work is documented most clearly at Shoofly Village (and also at what we posit is the subsequent home of the Payson people in the Tonto Basin). The diverse architectural traditions revealed in the layout of Shoofly Village has led us to hypothesize that the community comprised a series of previously autonomous and, possibly, ethnically diverse social groups. These groups probably maintained some of their autonomy while living at Shoofly Village, but our evidence also points to shared ceramic production and uniform subsistence routines. The possibility of ethnic diversity within a single region, and particularly within a single site, has not been widely discussed in the archaeological literature. I believe, however, that the evidence from Shoofly Village compels us to recognize that possibility. Too often, we have equated ceramic designs with ethnic or social identities, leading us to overlook the potential diversity in the majority of Southwestern communities and diverting research attention from what might be more meaningful approaches to ceramic designs, as suggested earlier in this chapter.

The possibility that ethnic diversity within a community characterized Southwestern lifeways has even more far-reaching implications when considering what must have existed in areas like the Tonto Basin during the fourteenth century if the people from Payson and other regions migrated there. It is not the subject of this book, but it is currently being investigated actively by Arizona State University and other research teams. Early investigations point out that some communities have distinctive cultural identities, yet they share in the use of the predominant decorated pottery. At the largest sites, there is some evidence of a diversity of social units reminiscent of Shoofly Village, but more closely integrated. It will still be years before definite conclusions are reached about the existence of ethnic diversity in the Tonto Basin and what social control mechanisms emerged to integrate it into a functioning society. Nevertheless, the implications of the patterns found at Shoofly Village should encourage researchers to consider the possibility of ethnic diversity within single communities, as well as across regions.

Archaeological projects like our own in the Payson region consume the energies and challenge the minds of many individuals. Tremendous quantities of objects are recovered and endless reams of information are recorded. While the project is going on, and for years after the trowels are put away, students and scholars pour over this information and attempt to describe prehistoric life as they believe it existed in the region. They also ponder broader questions of cultural change and stability and the very nature of human existence. As with most other

projects, ours has filled an important gap in the prehistory of the Southwest and has provided a vivid picture of life in this scenic portion of
Arizona. Our most valuable contributions, however, are not the questions we have answered nor the details of early lifeways we have provided but the new issues we have raised based on what the prehistoric
people of Payson have left behind. Simply summarized, three characteristics stand out from our investigations of twelfth-century Payson:
autonomy, mobility, and ethnic diversity. The pervasiveness and importance of these characteristics at Shoofly Village and among the people
of the region are not easily agreed upon by researchers, even among our
own team. Having brought these issues into clearer focus for scholars to
examine with the evidence of prehistory, however, we have enriched the
archaeological record for those who follow us, and perhaps we have
enriched the more general inquiry into our own existence.

APPENDIX 1: Radiocarbon Dates from the Payson Area

Site	Wood Material	Context	Sample #	Date B.P.	Calibrated Date A.D.**	1 Sigma Date Range A.D.
Shoofly	Beam?	E113 N124 6-13	SMU-1972	850 ± 30	1195, 1196, 1208	1159–1222
Shoofly	Beam	E113 N124 4-1	WSU-3489	900 ± 50	1133, 1136, 1156	1031–1209
Shoofly	Beam	E130 N125 5-6	SMU-1975	760 ± 30	1263	1233–1278
Shoofly	Fuel	E130 N125 7-15	BETA-23121	260 ± 80	1648	1516–1955
Shoofly	Beam	E130 N125 3-4	WSU-3491	1065 ± 90	984	887–1024
Shoofly	Post	E89 N165 2-16	SMU-1977	810 ± 40	1223	1193–1262
Shoofly	Post/Beam	E76 N114 2-1	BETA-23328	770 ± 60	1261	1214–1280
Shoofly	Post?	E91 N70 2-6	BETA-23118	650 ± 70	1296, 1375	1278–1393
Shoofly	Fuel?	E129 N174 5-15	BETA-23120	1,030 ± 100	997	894–1151
Shoofly	Fuel?	E134 N114 6-30	BETA-23122	790 ± 50	1257	1210–1277
Shoofly	Beam	E134 N114 6-9	WSU-3488	810 ± 50	1223	1164–1275
Shoofly	Post	E123 N158 1-10	WSU-3487	1,030 ± 100	997	894–1151
Shoofly	Roof?	E97 N85 4-5	WSU-3490	995 ± 70	1005, 1006, 1020	983–1152
532	Fuel	Rm. 2 2-0	WSU-3492	1,040 ± 80	995	897–1146
532	Post	Pithouse 1	WSU-3494	1,355 ± 80	659	609– 766
532	?	Rm. 6 3-0	WSU-3496	220 ± 70	1659	1639–1955
520	Fuel	E44 N24 3-0	WSU-3493	360 ± 120	1490	1430–1650

491	Structure #1	Post?	WSU-3495	1,430 ± 80	639	543– 662
246	TU #1	Post	SMU-1976	850 ± 30	1195, 1196, 1208	1159–1222
208	Pit Fill	Fuel	SMU-1974	1,020 ± 30	999	986–1022
619	Rm 3 In Hearth	Fuel	BETA 20124	890 ± 90	1158	1022–1256
620	Rm 15 In Hearth/Pit	Fuel	BETA 23126	680 ± 50	1282	1277–1385
620	Rm 9 In Floor*	Post	BETA 23127	820 ± 55	1219	1161–1262
620	Rm 23 In Hearth	Fuel	BETA 23325	690 ± 80	1281	1260–1388
620	TU 15 Midden	Fuel?	BETA 23326	160 ± 90	1678, 1739, 1804, 1938, 1955	1650–1955
630	Rm 2 In Hearth	Fuel	BETA 23129	710 ± 80	1280	1257–1385
635	Rm 3 Floor Fill	Beam	BETA 23130	850 ± 60	1195, 1196, 1208	1068–1258
637	Roasting Pit Fill*	Fuel	BETA 23131	720 ± 70	1279	1257–1377
639	Roasting Pit #3 Fill	Fuel	BETA 23132	730 ± 70	1278	1227–1285
647	Rm 2 Floor Fill*	Beam	BETA 23133	600 ± 60	1326, 1353, 1363, 1365, 1389	1284–1410
647	Rm 7 Midden	Fuel?	BETA 23327	770 ± 70	1261	1210–1281
648	Structure 5 Floor Fill	Beam?	BETA 23134	820 ± 100	1219	1043–1280
656	Roasting Pit Fill	Fuel	BETA 23135	420 ± 60	1443	1428–1492
AZ 0:11:1	Rm 1 Floor Fill	Fuel	BETA 23234	900 ± 90	1133, 1136, 1156	1020–1224

Source: Adapted from Lindauer 1991b.

*Contexts also dated by archaeomagnetism.

**Calibrated according to Stuiver and Becker 1986

APPENDIX 2:   Payson Area Archaeomagnetic Dating Information

Site	Location	Context	Sample #	Mean Sample Declination	Mean Sample Inclination
52	Rm 3, Hearth Burned	Room	AR:03:12:04:52-1	9.87	54.48
138	Rm 1, Hearth Burned	Room	AR:03:12:04:138-1	353.32	58.99
491	Pithouse #2 Hearth	Room	AR:03:12:04:491-1	5.54	52.44
532	Rm 5, Hearth Unburned	Unburned Room	AR:03:12:04:632-1	6.65	52.74
Shoofly	E87 N81 Plaza Hearth		AZ :0:11:6 (ASU)-1	0.53	54.18
Shoofly	E113 N124 Wall	Room Burned	AZ :0:11:6 (ASU)-2	18.89	65.38
Shoofly	E113 N124 Hearth	Room Burned	AZ :0:11:6 (ASU)-3	305.27	72.70
Shoofly	E123 N158 Later Hearth	Room Unburned	AZ :0:11:6 (ASU)-4	346.19	69.93
Shoofly	E123 N158 Lower Hearth	Room Unburned	AZ :0:11:6 (ASU)-5	357.46	54.95
620	Rm 6, Hearth Unburned	Room	AR:03:12:04:620-1	349.47	54.35
620	Rm 9, Hearth Burned	Room*	AR:03:12:04:620-2	353.17	60.03
620	Rm 18, Hearth Un-burned	Room	AR:03:12:04:620-3	355.04	62.36
620	Rm 8, Hearth Unburned	Room	AR:03:12:04:620-4	358.33	55.77
624	Hearth Unburned	Room	AR:03:12:04:624-1	358.58	55.61
632	Rm 2, Hearth Unburned	Room	AR:03:12:04:632-1	200.22	62.15
632	Rm 1, Hearth Unburned	Room	AR:03:12:04:632-2	352.98	61.53
637	Roasting Pit	Pit Wall*	AR:03:12:04:637-1	351.87	57.44
647	Rm 9	Burned Rm*	AR:03:12:04:647-1	353.64	61.61

Source: Adapted from Lindauer 1991b.
*Contexts also dated by radiocarbon 14.

ample aleolattitude	Sample Paleolongitude	Mean Sample Alpha 95	Mean Precisions	Ep Degrees	Em Degrees	Date Ranges A.D.
.85	330.52	2.78	N.A.	2.76	3.92	None Possible
2.33	206.63	3.48	N.A.	3.87	5.19	925–1025, 1150–1450
5.23	352.21	3.90	N.A.	3.69	5.37	680–735, 845–1000
4.40	346.26	3.21	N.A.	3.05	4.43	680–725, 845–1000
9.39	294.31	7.98	N.A.	7.87	11.20	680–800, 835–1025, 1300–1450
0.64	290.02	2.29	N.A.	3.02	3.72	None Possible
6.93	209.52	13.07	N.A.	20.66	23.44	Sample Not Demagnitized
8.17	226.46	5.44	N.A.	8.04	9.36	None Possible
7.60	189.19	5.64	N.A.	5.67	7.99	680–800, 1300–1450, 900–1025
1.38	163.37	1.21	1336.64	1.21	1.72	Off Curve
1.46	209.96	2.37	374.08	2.69	3.57	1000–1075, 1175–1375
9.90	227.79	3.20	204.71	3.81	4.90	1000–1050, 1250–1375
7.97	209.90	3.33	171.94	3.43	4.82	920–1020, 1375–Post-1450
7.73	216.19	5.46	64.30	5.72	7.99	Pre-700–725, 900–1040, 1200–Post-1450
9.63	247.87	13.25	20.88			No Date, Poor Sample
8.90	215.28	3.13	194.76	3.63	4.67	1010–1100, 1200–1375
2.49	191.70	2.14	454.42	2.29	3.13	1000–1025, 1175–1250
0.96	216.02	3.45	176.25	4.12	5.41	975–1000, 1170–Post-1450

APPENDIX 3: Charred Plant Remains Recovered from Payson Area Sites

SITE	S.V.*	620	637	619	650	647	21	632	624	631	656	640	639
No. of Samples	N=74	N=17	N=4	N=3	N=3	N=8	N=2	N=2	N=1	N=1	N=1	N=2	N=4
PLANT TAXA													
Spring													
Agave	X												
Mustard family	X												
Spring/Summer													
Globemallow	X			X									
Manzanita	X		X										X
Juncus	X												
Summer/Fall													
Aster	X				X								
Cheno-am	X	X		X	X								
Purslane	X	X											
Grass family	X												
Juniper	X				X						X		
Unidentifiable	X	X			X							X	
Unknown	X	X			X					X			

Fall

Maize	X	X	X	X	X	X	X	X
Squash	X						X	X
Cotton	X							
Bean	X			X				
Walnut	X	X						
WOOD								
Gymnosperm	X	X			X	X		
Juniper	X	X	X		X	X		X
Pine	X							
Oak	X				X			X
Hardwood	X	X			X			
Willow/ Cottonwood	X							
Sycamore	X							
Unidentifiable	X	X		X	X	X	X	X

Source: Adapted from Miller 1991.

*S.V. - Shoofly Village.

179

APPENDIX 4:   Vertebrate Taxa Recovered from Payson Area

Class Amphibia	Amphibians
Class Reptilia	Reptiles
Order Testudinata	Turtles and tortoises
Order Squamata (Suborder	
Serpentes)	Snakes
Class Aves	Birds
Order Falconiformes	
Family Accipitridae	
Buteo lagopus (Pontoppidan)	Rough-legged hawk
Class Mammalia	Mammals
Order Lagomorpha	
Family Leporidae	
Lepus spp.	Jackrabbit
Sylvilagus spp.	Cottontail
Order Rodentia	Rodents
Family Sciuridae	
Sciurus spp.	Tree squirrels
Order Artiodactyla	Artiodactyls
Family Cervidae	
Cervus canadensis (Erxleben)	Elk
Odocoileus spp.	Deer
Family Bovidae	Cows, sheep, and allies

Source: Adapted from Atwell and Eshbaugh 1991.

Glossary

absolute dating: A series of methods for determining the date of archaeological material based on natural scientific techniques such as radiocarbon, archeomagnetism, or dendrochronology.

alluvium: Clay, silt, sand, or gravel deposited by running water. An *alluvial valley* is usually a flat plain adjacent to a river, built up during floods. Often this land is particularly suited for farming since it has access to river water either from flooding or from human-induced irrigation. An *alluvial fan* is a ridge-like deposit where a stream emerges from a gorge out onto a plain or where a tributary stream joins the main stream.

arable land: Soil that is fit for crop cultivation. It usually includes adequate soil composition to nourish plants, sufficient soil depth, and access to water.

archaeological survey: A systematic investigation of a defined area to detect the presence of archaeological sites or other evidence of past activities. This is often accomplished by walking over the terrain, but also can be done by vehicle or even by airplane. Records of each site discovered often include descriptions of artifacts exposed on the site's surface, any visible architectural features, and local environmental conditions.

archaeomagnetic dating: A method for dating archaeological deposits based on the fact that the earth's magnetic poles have shifted location with the passage of time, a phenomenon known as "procession." When clay is sufficiently heated, the iron minerals in it align themselves with the magnetic poles. Archaeologists can record the position of a baked clay piece in the ground (usually from a hearth or burned building), remove pieces, make a laboratory measurement of the magnetic orientation of the sample, and compare that orientation to known magnetic pole positions through time.

Archaic period: In the American Southwest as well as in many other regions this usually refers to the broad period of time that precedes agriculture and settled village life. New evidence on early agriculture in the American Southwest complicates this definition, but conventionally it refers to a period from about 3000–4000 B.C. to about A.D. 700.

arroyo: A watercourse in an arid region. Arroyo can refer to an active creek or stream, but it usually means a gully formed by a periodic stream that is dry for much of the year.

artifact: Any object produced or modified by humans. Archaeologists usually use this term to indicate the tools, containers, manufacturing residues, and sometimes even the built environments of ancient peoples.

brownware: A general designation for a wide range of undecorated pottery types that comprise the majority of vessels made by the prehistoric peoples of central Arizona and other regions. Usually the manufacturing techniques, the vessel shapes, and the mineral inclusions in the clays allow archaeologists to subdivide this broad category into many types that appear to have been made in separate localities of the Southwest.

buffware: A category of pottery that was fired in an oxidizing atmosphere causing it to have a buff or sometimes pinkish color. Buffware vessels are best known from the lowland desert regions of the Hohokam where they were often decorated with designs in a reddish paint.

burnished: A technique in the manufacture of pottery in which a hard object, such as a stone or smoothed sherd, is rubbed over the surface of a clay vessel after it has dried in order to seal its surface and create a low polish.

chaparral: An ecological community composed largely of shrubbery. In central Arizona, this often occurs above the lowland deserts but below the woodland elevations. It is dominated by evergreen oaks, manzanita, and various "brush" varieties.

check dam: A stone barrier constructed by prehistoric farmers to control water runoff. When water runoff occurred on natural drainages on hill slopes, some could be held behind these dams, leading to the deposition of clay or silt and often a higher retention of groundwater.

chipped stone: A tool made by striking a stone with a hard object so that flakes are detached, shaping the stone and flakes for use. The result may be a small projectile point, a sharp cutting implement, or a blunt scraping tool, as well as countless other artifacts.

Clovis period: The earliest period of human habitation in the American Southwest, named after the Clovis point, a characteristic lance point that has been found at widely distributed early hunting sites. The beginning of this period is debated, but it can be placed roughly at 8000 B.C. to about 3000 B.C., the beginning of the Archaic period.

Colorado Plateau: The upland region that extends north and east from the Mogollon Rim across northern Arizona, and into Utah, Colorado, and New Mexico. It coincides roughly with the homeland of the prehistoric Anasazi culture.

complex society: Archaeologists use this term to refer to a group of people that is organized in a hierarchical fashion in which there are status positions that restrict access to resources and authority. There are different levels of complexity, varying from a simple chiefdom to a modern nation state.

contract archaeology: Archaeological work done by contract with a developer or government agency usually because the archaeological work is required by law. Various state and federal laws require a professional archaeological exploration of sites that will be impacted by public projects, such as road or dam construction. Often this involves the excavation of sites to retrieve their information before they are destroyed.

cortex: The rough, naturally weathered surface of a rock. In the course of shaping a chipped stone implement from a rock, some flakes—and even some finished tools—may retain a portion of the cortex, indicating that they were originally from the outer part of the rock.

creek zone: The stream valleys and adjacent ridges in the Payson-Star Valley area. It is assumed that the prehistoric peoples who lived in this zone relied in large part on the agricultural productivity of the better watered, deeper soil valleys, in contrast to upland zone dwellers.

cross-dating: A technique for dating cultural remains by using an artifact of a known date that is found among those remains. Whenever we find a distinctive artifact whose date of manufacture is known, such as a specific category of painted pottery, we can infer that the deposits in which it was found are of the same date. This is one of the most commonly used methods for dating archaeological deposits, but it must be used cautiously because of a variety of intervening variables, such as we described for the decorated ceramics found in the Payson-Star Valley area.

culture history: When archaeologists attempt to reconstruct the sequence of events that occurred in a region during prehistoric times, they call it a culture history. Among the elements of a culture history are the characteristics of settlements, the nature of subsistence and technology, and the population estimates for each period a region was occupied.

cultural tradition: One of the basic principles of anthropology is that groups of people throughout all time periods and in all parts of the world tend to develop their own sets of practices and beliefs that provide them with an identity and distinguish them from other groups. These characteristics, which may include rituals, house forms, subsistence pursuits, artifact decoration, etc., are likely to change over time and vary among neighboring communities, but there are basic patterns that allow the groups (and the anthropologist) to distinguish one cultural tradition from another. In the prehistoric Southwest, archaeologists have identified a number of major cultural traditions. Primary among these are the Anasazi, Mogollon, Hohokam, Sinagua, and Salado.

daub: Clay applied in layers, most often in the construction of wood beam and clay walls. Daub used to seal the walls against wind and water also serves as insulation.

dendrochronology: A method for dating the year when a tree found at an archaeological site was originally cut down. It is based on the principle that annual tree rings vary in size with the amount of annual rainfall and that the sequence of these variations is unique, allowing archaeological samples to be matched against the master calibration chart to determine the age of the wood.

depositional history: Most artifacts and features in archaeological sites are buried. The nature of the deposits above and below them reveal their history and their relationship to objects and features laid down before and after. This is based on the "superimposition principle" of *stratigraphy*—that materials found at a lower point in a sequence of deposits were laid down before those above them.

dry farming: This refers to the cultivation and harvesting of crops—primarily corn in the Payson-Star Valley region—watered by rainfall and surface runoff alone. This is in contrast to *irrigation farming*, in which some of the requisite water for crops is brought to the fields through human effort.

ecofact: Remains such as animal bones or plant parts or pollen samples that provide information on the prehistoric diet and climate.

feature: This is any culturally altered locality, such as hearths, storage pits, burials, etc., within an archaeological site. The term implies that a feature is a built or modified place that has contents, such as artifacts, ecofacts, or residues of some activity.

field school: Practical training is an essential part of the academic career of all archaeology students. It is often achieved by attending a field school. A field school is a training situation usually focused around an excavation and/or archaeological survey where actual research is conducted by the students under the close supervision of professionals.

fill deposit: Abandoned locations of prehistoric activity are often covered over and filled by either natural or human induced forces. The material that covers a prehistoric surface is referred to as a fill deposit, especially when it is located within a delineated area, such as a room.

floor zone: The stratum or deposit that is identified as the primary living surface(s) of a room. It is assumed to have contained the artifacts, ecofacts, and features that were used by the inhabitants of that room, some of which may remain.

florescence: A term used by archaeologists to denote the period of greatest cultural achievement of a particular group of people. Florescence literally means "blossoming."

groundstone: Artifacts that were manufactured by abrading or grinding the stone into the desired shape. Groundstone tools are often used to grind various kinds of material. Milling stones (metates and manos) and pestles are the most common form of groundstone found in the Payson region.

hamlet: A small village composed of a few houses. In this volume, it is used to indicate an archaeological site that contained between six and forty rooms, although the actual community in residence at any one time used as few as six to ten rooms and involved an equivalent or lesser number of families.

hearth: A place where a fire was habitually made, often within a room. Hearths are sometimes carefully constructed with stone slabs lining the sides and bottom; in other instances, there is no evidence of special construction, but the place is repeatedly reused and the surrounding dirt is fire-hardened.

Hohokam: The name given to a very widespread group that inhabited the riverine areas of the southern Arizona deserts throughout much of prehistory. They effectively utilized irrigation for farming, which enabled them to support large populations, major construction works, and long-distance trading networks. Archaeological evidence of Hohokam influence or contact found in the Payson area includes red-painted buffware pottery, groundstone palettes, and a distinctive type of pithouse.

intrusive: Objects that were not made in the region where they were found. This may be determined, for example, by the presence of a distinctive type of design characteristic of a non-local culture or by raw materials that identify its place of origin to be far away. Such an object is often cited as evidence of trade, and sometimes it can aid in dating the archaeological deposit in which it was found. See: cross-dating

jacal: Lightly built mud and wood buildings or walls within buildings. Often the foundation of a prehistoric building in the Payson area was built of stone, but the superstructure was usually made of jacal.

laboratory processing: The cleaning, labeling, and preliminary categorization of artifacts, ecofacts, and other material that are collected during archaeological fieldwork.

lithics: All stone artifacts can be called "lithics," but archaeologists most often use the term to refer to chipped stone.

macrobotanical: The remains of seeds and other plant parts that can be seen with the unaided eye. They are recovered during archaeological fieldwork from the soil either by careful hand sorting or through a technique known as "flotation" in which excavated soil is immersed in a liquid and macrobotanical remains float to the surface. Macrobotanical remains are usually carbonized from burning; unburned plant remains decay very quickly and rarely survive at archaeological sites.

maize: A form of corn, the most extensively grown domestic plant of prehistoric North America.

mano: A hand-held stone used for grinding seed plants, such as corn, to make them more edible. Manos are shaped by grinding and are most often made of a coarse-grained stone, such as basalt or sandstone. See: metate

masonry architecture: Buildings or other features made entirely or in part of stone. In this volume, all stone construction is referred to as masonry, while in writing about more complex societies, some archaeologists restrict the use of this term to architecture in which the stones have been carefully shaped and fitted together.

mealing bin: Prehistoric peoples, as well as ethnographically known Indian groups, often allocated particular places within their houses or settlements for grinding food. These mealing bins usually contain one or more metates and accompanying manos, as well as the residues of food.

metate: The base stone used for grinding seeds, such as corn, to make them more edible. They are shaped into either flat slabs or troughs through chipping and grinding, and they are made of a coarse material, such as basalt or sandstone. A mano is moved back and forth across a stationary metate to grind seeds on the metate surface into a fine flour.

midden: A location where refuse is deposited in an ancient community. For archaeologists, these are areas that often contain dense accumulations of artifacts and ecofactual material. Sometimes middens are located away from the occupied area of a settlement and sometimes they are found in abandoned rooms that were used as receptacles for refuse.

Mogollon: A term used to describe the uplands of central Arizona, in particular, the escarpment or "rim" that demarcates the southern edge of the Colorado Plateau. The term appears to have come from the name of an early captain general of New Mexico. Archaeologists use the term Mogollon to refer to prehistoric groups that occupied eastern and north-central Arizona. These groups are characterized by their use of large pithouses (and eventually, surface rooms), as well as undecorated brown-ware pottery and distinctive black-on-white ceramics.

Mogollon Rim: the escarpment north of Payson that forms the southern edge of the Colorado Plateau. This rim is often called the Tonto Rim (as in this volume) and its abrupt elevation change creates a variety of climatic microzones in its vicinity.

paddle and anvil: A technique for constructing pottery vessels used in the Payson area and in most of southern and central Arizona. The vessel is shaped from a lump of wet clay with the aid of two flat objects that are used to draw the clay up and flatten the vessel sides. Sometimes the technique is used to finish an already formed vessel.

Paleoindian: This refers to the early inhabitants of North America, including the Payson region. These early Indian groups are not well understood, but some researchers believe these people followed the remaining big game during the period after the last Ice Age until about 3000 B.C.

petrography: The identification of the mineral content and structure of rocks and mineral-containing composite materials, such as ceramics. This is usually done to identify the characteristics of the material and possibly its place of origin. Petrography in its most simple form can be accomplished with a simple hand lens, but most often it is done using high-powered microscopes and other scientific instruments.

pithouse: Buildings that are constructed in excavated depressions in the ground making the living surface lower than the surrounding ground. They are most often oval or a rounded rectangular shape and made of mud and timbers (jacal), sometimes with a stone foundation.

plainware: Undecorated ceramics that comprise the majority of all ceramics in the world. The only type of ceramics manufactured in the Payson region prehistorically were plainwares.

polychrome: Ceramics that have been decorated using more than one color. Polychrome decoration is a relatively recent development in the Southwest and usually indicates cultures of the thirteenth century or later.

posthole: Because most unburned organic material deteriorates quickly, archaeologists rarely recover the wooden posts that supported buildings, but they do find the holes that these posts were put into. Postholes are identified by differences in the color and texture of the soil or by remnants of the post itself.

pot bust: The broken but potentially reconstructible pieces of a ceramic vessel more or less in the location it was left. Ceramic vessels are frequently broken when a room is abandoned or collapses.

pothunter: An individual who disrupts archaeological sites to collect objects. Archaeological sites are sometimes vandalized in unscientific searches for objects that are deemed desirable or even valuable. Despite laws prohibiting this activity, it continues to be one of the major threats to the preservation of the archaeological record.

Precambrian: This term refers to the very earliest period of geological history and to the rock layers that were formed at that time; before life on earth.

prehistoric: All cultures and objects that existed before the introduction of writing. In North America, this is interpreted to mean all societies before A.D. 1492. Although most American Indians did not come into contact with literate groups until much later, this date is maintained as the demarcation between prehistory and history (although in Arizona, we use the term "proto-history" to refer to the period between A.D. 1492 and European contact in any particular locality).

pressure flaking: A method for shaping chipped stone tools by pressing a hard object, such as antler or rock, against the potential tool in order to remove flakes from it in a carefully controlled way. This can result in very precisely shaped implements.

projectile point: A chipped stone piece with a pointed shape, assumed to have been used as an arrow or lance tip. Projectile points are numerous at many North American archaeological sites, including those in the Payson area. Sometimes the shape or method of manufacture is sufficiently distinctive to allow the archaeologist to identify the period or the region of origin.

protohistoric: The period between A.D. 1492 and when any particular indigenous North American group came into sustained contact with Europeans.

pueblo: A word borrowed from Spanish where it means building or town. Southwestern archaeologists, however, use the term to refer to above-surface, rectangular, contiguous buildings. The Anasazi settlements beginning in the eighth century A.D. are the model for defining pueblo architecture, but the core roomblock at Shoofly is also an example of pueblo architecture.

Quaternary: This refers to a geologically defined period comprising the Holocene (the last 10,000 years) and the Pleistocene (2 million years before that). It is roughly coincident with the existence of the genus *Homo*.

radiocarbon dating: A method for estimating the age of organic material. A certain percentage of the carbon in atmospheric gasses is radioactive. Once that radioactive carbon (called carbon-14) is made part of an organism and the organism dies, the carbon undergoes radioactive decay at a predictable rate, resulting in a steadily decreasing proportion of radioactive carbon in the dead organism. Hence, samples of organic material can be analyzed and dates suggested for when a tree was cut down or a seed harvested. This method is also called "charcoal dating" and "carbon-14 dating."

ramada: A lightly built structure, sometimes with fewer than four walls. These may have served as houses at short-term settlements or as specialized structures within settlements that have more substantial buildings as well.

random sampling: A mathematically based procedure for selecting some objects or an area from a larger group or area that reduces the biases inherent in purposeful selection. It is often used to reduce a researcher's tendency to favor certain portions of unanalyzed data or sites. A modified form of random sampling was used to select the location for the initial test excavations at Shoofly Village.

redware: At the beginning of the thirteenth century, certain Southwestern societies began to produce ceramic vessels with an overall coating rich in iron that gave them a red color after firing in an oxidizing atmosphere. Some of these had a solid red color (e.g., Tonto redware), and others were decorated on top of the red coating with one or more colors before firing (e.g., St. Johns redware).

retouch: A method, usually involving pressure flaking, or finely shaping or sharpening chipped stone tools.

rim of a vessel: The upper edge of a bowl or jar. Discovery of a rim is important for an archaeologist because, from even a small rim piece, it is often possible to estimate the size and shape of the entire vessel.

roasting pit: A considerable amount of cooking was accomplished by placing the food in or over a fire in a roughly formed pit that is less well-defined than a hearth. Roasting pits were especially useful for cooking large pieces of meat.

roomblock: A group of rooms built together and often attached to other groups to form a large settlement. In the Payson area, roomblocks are not as tightly clustered as at many Anasazi sites, but they are identifiable as separate clusters nevertheless.

rubble-core walls: A technique for building thick walls in which well-laid courses of stone form the outer surfaces of the wall, and the interior "core" is filled with unshaped stones.

Salado: The name given by archaeologists to some of the prehistoric Indian groups that lived between A.D. 1100 and A.D. 1400 in central Arizona. Distinguishing characteristics include distinctive ceramics (classified as Gila Polychrome), the presence of elevated constructions called platform mounds, and enclosure walls around some settlements.

scatter: Artifacts on the surface of a site. Often an unexcavated site is referred to as an "artifact scatter" when there is no evidence of architecture.

shatter: In the process of manufacturing chipped stone tools, irregular pieces are broken off. The flatter, more intact pieces are referred to as flakes, and the remainder are called shatter.

sherd: A piece of a broken ceramic vessel is called a sherd or potsherd. Because fired ceramic material disintegrates very slowly, potsherds are well represented in the archaeological record.

Sinagua: The name given by archaeologists to one group of prehistoric Indians who lived in central and north-central Arizona.

slip: A fluid mixture of clay and water that may be applied to the surface of a vessel before firing in order to change its characteristics, such as color, hardness, or porosity.

smudging: A process in which carbon is applied to the surface of a vessel during or after the firing process. This appears to change the porosity, as well as the appearance, of a vessel.

Sonoran Desert: The biotic community that exists in southern and central Arizona and adjacent northern Mexico. Saguaro cactus and palo verde trees are among the plants that characterize the region.

soundings: Small exploratory excavations that are used to probe different areas of an archaeological site or to sample depths below current excavations. These can be used to learn efficiently about broad areas of a settlement or to determine where to locate larger excavation units.

stratigraphy: The superimposed layers of soil, fill, and living surfaces that an archaeological site comprises. The careful excavation of a site by successive stratigraphic levels allows archaeologists to associate artifacts and features that may have been used together, as well as provide a relative chronology for those items.

subrectangular: A four-sided shape that has rounded corners but roughly straight sides. In the Payson area, it is a very common shape for free-standing structures.

subsistence: The sources of food utilized by the inhabitants of a settlement. In the Payson region during the period of interest in this volume, corn was the main food, supplemented by a variety of other domesticated plants and wild plant and animal resources.

temper: Small particles of material mixed with clay to improve the qualities of the finished ceramic vessel. Crushed rocks, sand, or crushed potsherds were commonly used as temper in central Arizona.

Tonto Basin: The large valley in central Arizona where Tonto Creek joins the Salt River. It is located directly south of the Payson area, and people may have moved between the two regions during prehistory.

Tonto Rim: This is the name often used for the southern escarpment of the Colorado Plateau, especially in the Payson-Star Valley area. Although most maps use the name Mogollon Rim for the entire feature, use of the term Tonto Rim for one particular section was popularized by Zane Grey in several of his novels.

trade ware: Archaeologists believe that substantial quantities of ceramics were transported from their place of manufacture to be used by inhabitants of other regions. These trade wares often have a characteristic decoration or mineral composition that allow archaeologists to identify their time and place of origin.

upland zone: In this volume, upland zone is used to refer to areas that are more distant from the major water drainages of the region than areas that we have called the creek zone. The upland zone consists of ridges, mesa tops, and mountain slopes that normally would have less cultivable land nearby than the creek zone had.

x-ray florescence: A method to identify the relative proportions of certain chemical elements in a material. Using special laboratory equipment, an artifact is exposed to x-rays. The different chemical elements in the artifact then fluoresce in characteristic ways that allow a researcher to see what elements are present and in what quantities. Archaeologists often use this technique to characterize the composition of obsidian or clay in order to determine its place of origin.

Background Reading

Ceram, C. W.
1971   *The First American: A Story of North American Archaeology.* New American Library, New York.

Cordell, Linda S.
1984   *The Prehistory of the Southwest.* Academic Press, New York.

Crown, Patricia L., and W. James Judge (editors)
1991   *Chaco and Hohokam: Prehistoric Regional Systems in the American Southwest.* School of American Research Press, Santa Fe.

Dozier, Edward P.
1970   *The Pueblo Indians of North America.* Holt, Rinehart and Winston, New York.

Gumerman, George J. (editor)
1991   *Exploring the Hohokam: Prehistoric Desert Peoples of the American Southwest.* University of New Mexico Press, Albuquerque.

Haury, Emil W.
1976   *The Hohokam: Desert Farmers and Craftsmen.* University of Arizona Press, Tucson.

Jennings, Jesse D. (editor)
1978   *Ancient Native Americans.* W. H. Freeman and Co., San Francisco.

Kidder, Alfred Vincent
1924   *An Introduction to the Study of Southwestern Archaeology.* Yale University Press, New Haven.

Longacre, William A. (editor)
1970   *Reconstructing Prehistoric Pueblo Societies.* University of New Mexico Press, Albuquerque.

Minnis, Paul E., and Charles L. Redman (editors)
   1990   *Perspectives on Southwestern Prehistory*. Westview Press, Boulder, Colorado.
Willey, Gordon R., and Jeremy A. Sabloff
   1980   *A History of American Archaeology*, 2nd edition. W. H. Freeman and Co., San Francisco.

References Cited

Abbott, David R.
1981   An Evaluation of the Behavioral Significance of Two Low-Density Artifact Scatters from Payson, Arizona. Master's thesis, Department of Anthropology, Arizona State University, Tempe.

Adams, Elmer D.
1968   *Soil Survey and Interpretations of the Soils in the Payson Area, Gila County, Arizona, June 1968, A Special Report.* Prepared by U. S. Department of Agriculture, Soil Conservation Service, in cooperation with the Payson Sanitary District and the Tonto Soil Conservation District, Phoenix.

Adams, Robert McC.
1978   Strategies of Maximization, Stability, and Resilience in Mesopotamian Society, Settlement, and Agriculture. *Proceedings of the American Philosophical Society* 122:329–35.

Atwell, Karen A., and David C. Eshbaugh
1991   Faunal Remains. In *The Archaeology of Star Valley, Arizona: Variation in Small Communities,* edited by Owen Lindauer, Ronna J. Bradley, and Charles L. Redman, pp. 372–79. Anthropological Field Studies No. 24. Department of Anthropology, Arizona State University, Tempe.

Atwell, Karen A., and Susan Menkhus
1991   Human Osetological Remains. In *The Archaeology of Star Valley, Arizona: Variation in Small Communities,* edited by Owen Lindauer, Ronna J. Bradley, and Charles L. Redman, pp. 404–11. Anthropological Field Studies No. 24, Department of Anthropology, Arizona State University, Tempe.

Basso, Keith H.
     1983   Western Apache. In *Handbook of North American Indians, Vol. 10:*
             Southwest, edited by Alfonso Ortiz, pp. 462–88. Smithsonian
             Institution, Washington, D.C.

Bradley, Ronna J.
     1991a   Chipped Stone Artifacts. In *The Archaeology of Star Valley, Arizona:*
             Variation in Small Communities, edited by Owen Lindauer, Ronna
             J. Bradley, and Charles L. Redman, pp. 411–37. Anthropologi-
             cal Field Studies No. 24, Department of Anthropology, Arizona
             State University, Tempe.

     1991b   Site AR-03-12-04-620 (TNF). In *The Archaeology of Star Valley,*
             Arizona: Variation in Small Communities, edited by Owen Lindauer,
             Ronna J. Bradley, and Charles L. Redman, pp. 154–206.
             Anthropological Field Studies No. 24, Department of Anthropol-
             ogy, Arizona State University, Tempe.

Braidwood, Linda
     1953   *Digging Beyond the Tigris.* Henry Schuman, New York.

Broderick, Howard
     1973   Soil Resource Inventory, Tonto National Forest, Payson Ranger
             District. Manuscript on file, Tonto National Forest, Phoenix.

Brown, David E., and Charles H. Lowe
     1980   *Biotic Communities of the Southwest.* General Technical Report
             RM-78, Rocky Mountain Forest and Range Experiment Station,
             U.S. Department of Agriculture, Forest Service.

Bruder, J. Simon, and Richard Ciolek-Torrello
     1987   Ceramic Analysis. In *Archaeology of the Mazatzal Piedmont, Central*
             Arizona, edited by R. Ciolek-Torrello, pp. 82–114. Museum of
             Northern Arizona Research Paper 33, Vol. 1. Museum of North-
             ern Arizona Press, Flagstaff.

Burton, James H.
     1988   Plainware Provenience and Typology: A Trace Mineral Study.
             Paper presented at the 53rd annual meeting of the Society for
             American Archaeology, Phoenix.

     1991   Geology. In *The Archaeology of Star Valley, Arizona: Variation in Small*
             Communities, edited by Owen Lindauer, Ronna J. Bradley, and
             Charles L. Redman, pp. 21–27. Anthropological Field Studies
             No. 24, Department of Anthropology, Arizona State University,
             Tempe.

Buskirk, Winfred
     1949   *Western Apache Subsistence Economy.* Ph.D. dissertation, Depart-
             ment of Anthropology, University of New Mexico, Albuquerque.

1986   *The Western Apache: Living with the Land before 1950.* University of
        Oklahoma Press, Norman.

Christie, Agatha
1946   *Come, Tell Me How You Live.* Dodd, Mead and Company, New
        York.

Cordell, Linda
1984   *The Prehistory of the Southwest.* Academic Press, New York.

Crown, Patricia L., and Ronald L. Bishop
1987   Convergence in Ceramic Manufacturing Traditions in the Late
        Prehistoric Southwest. Paper presented at the 52nd annual meet-
        ing of the Society for American Archaeology, Toronto.

Crown, Patricia L., and W. James Judge (editors)
1991   *Chaco and Hohokam: Prehistoric Regional Systems in the American South-
        west.* School of American Research Press, Santa Fe.

Davis, Whitney
1990   Style and History in Art History. In *The Uses of Style in Archaeology,*
        edited by Margaret W. Conkey and Christine A. Hastorf, pp. 18–
        31. Cambridge University Press, Cambridge.

Denten, Branwen
1985   The Ceramic Figurine Fragments from Shoofly Village, 1985.
        Manuscript on file, Department of Anthropology, Arizona State
        University, Tempe.

Dittert, Alfred E., Jr.
1975   A Preliminary Report on the 1975 Season Investigations, Payson
        Ranger District, Tonto National Forest, Phoenix. Manuscript on
        file, Tonto National Forest, Phoenix.

1976   The 1976 Season: Archaeological Studies in the Payson Ranger
        District, Tonto National Forest, Arizona. Manuscript on file,
        Tonto National Forest, Phoenix.

Duennwald, Gabriel
1986   Preliminary Analysis of Plainware Ceramics from Shoofly Vil-
        lage, Arizona. Master's publishable paper, Department of
        Anthropology, Arizona State University, Tempe.

Eighmy, Jeffrey, L., and Randall H. McGuire
1988   *Archaeomagnetic Dates and the Hohokam Phase Sequence.* Colorado
        State University, Archaeomagnetic Lab, Technical Series No. 3.
        Fort Collins, Colorado.

Elson, Mark D.
   1989   Recent Research in the Northern Tonto Basin. *Data Recovery for the State Route 87/Rye Creek Project, Technical Report No. 89-3,* edited by Mark D. Elson and William H. Doelle, pp. 1–7. Institute for American Research, Tucson.

Elson, Mark D., and James Gundersen
   1992   *X-Ray Diffraction Results of the Sourcing of Argillite Artifacts from the Sites of Shoofly Village (AZ O:11:6), AZ O:11:44, and AZ O:15:12.* Center for Desert Archaeology Technical Report No. 92–93, Tucson.

Eshbaugh, David C.
   1988   Faunal Remains from the Shoofly Village Ruins, Arizona. Master's publishable paper, Department of Anthropology, Arizona State University, Tempe.

Fish, Suzanne K., Paul R. Rish, and John H. Madsen
   1985   A Preliminary Analysis of Hohokam Settlement and Agriculture in the Northern Tucson Basin. *Proceedings of the 1983 Hohokam Symposium,* edited by A. E. Dittert, Jr., and D. E. Dove, pp. 75–100. Phoenix Chapter, Arizona Archaeological Society, Phoenix.

Gifford, Edward W.
   1936   The Northeastern and Western Yavapai. *University of California Publication in American Archaeology and Ethnology* 34:247–354.

Goodwin, Grenville
   1942   *The Social Organization of the Western Apache.* University of Arizona Press, Tucson.

Granger, Byrd H.
   1960   *Will C. Barnes' Arizona Place Names.* University of Arizona Press, Tucson.

Gregory, Michael M.
   1989   A Pollen Analysis of Shoofly Village Ruins, Payson, Arizona. Master's thesis, Department of Anthropology, Arizona State University, Tempe.

   1991a   Pollen Remains. In *The Archaeology of Star Valley, Arizona: Variation in Small Communities,* edited by Owen Lindauer, Ronna J. Bradley, and Charles L. Redman, pp. 393–404. Anthropological Field Studies No. 24, Department of Anthropology, Arizona State University, Tempe.

   1991b   Site AR-03-12-04-652 (TNF). In *The Archaeology of Star Valley, Arizona: Variation in Small Communities,* edited by Owen Lindauer, Ronna J. Bradley, and Charles L. Redman, pp. 325–35. Anthropological Field Studies No. 24, Department of Anthropology, Arizona State University, Tempe.

Gumerman, George J. (editor)
1991   *Exploring the Hohokam: Prehistoric Desert Peoples of the American South-west.* University of New Mexico Press, Albuquerque.

Hammack, Laurens C.
1969   Highway Salvage Excavations in the Upper Tonto Basin, Arizona. *The Kiva* 34:132–75.

Haury, Emil W.
1976   *The Hohokam: Desert Farmers and Craftsmen.* University of Arizona Press, Tucson.

Hoffman, Chris
1985   An Analysis of the Materials in the Walls of Shoofly Village. Manuscript on file, Department of Anthropology, Arizona State University, Tempe.

Hohmann, John W.
1988a   Adjustments to Our Model. In *Continuing Studies in Payson Prehistory,* edited by John W. Hohmann and Charles L. Redman, pp. 22–49. Anthropological Field Studies No. 21, Office of Cultural Resource Management, Department of Anthropology, Arizona State University, Tempe.

1988b   Scorpion Rock Ruin, Site AR-03-12-04-532 (TNF). In *Continuing Studies in Payson Prehistory,* edited by John W. Hohmann and Charles L. Redman, pp. 50–97. Anthropological Field Studies No. 21, Office of Cultural Resource Management, Department of Anthropology, Arizona State University, Tempe.

1988c   Horton Rock Shelter, Site AR-03-12-04-520 (TNF). In *Continuing Studies in Payson Prehistory,* edited by John W. Hohmann and Charles L. Redman, pp. 22–49. Anthropological Field Studies No. 21, Office of Cultural Resource Management, Department of Anthropology, Arizona State University, Tempe.

Hohmann, John W., and Karen A. Atwell
1988   Deer Jaw Ruin, Site AR-03-12-04-208 (TNF). In *Continuing Studies in Payson Prehistory,* edited by John W. Hohmann and Charles L. Redman, pp. 136–91. Anthropological Field Studies No. 21, Office of Cultural Resource Management, Department of Anthropology, Arizona State University, Tempe.

Hohmann, John W., and Michael M. Gregory
1988   Pinyon Ruin, Site AR-03-12-04-246 (TNF). In *Continuing Studies in Payson Prehistory,* edited by John W. Hohmann and Charles L. Redman, pp. 192–224. Anthropological Field Studies No. 21, Office of Cultural Resource Management, Department of Anthropology, Arizona State University, Tempe.

Hohmann, John W., and Linda B. Hohmann
1986   Mud Springs Ruin, Site AR-03-12-04-52 (TNF). In *Small Site Variability in the Payson Region: The FLEX Land Exchange*, edited by Charles L. Redman and John W. Hohmann, pp. 189–208. Anthropological Field Studies No. 11. Office of Cultural Resource Management, Department of Anthropology, Arizona State University, Tempe.

Hohmann, John W., and Charles L. Redman (editors)
1988   *Continuing Studies in Payson Prehistory.* Anthropological Field Studies No. 21, Office of Cultural Resource Management, Department of Anthropology, Arizona State University, Tempe.

Huckell, Bruce B.
1978   *The Oxbow Hill-Payson Project: Archaeological Excavations South of Payson, Arizona.* Arizona State Museum Contribution to Highway Salvage Archeology in Arizona No. 48. Arizona State Museum, Tucson.

Ivanhoe, Francis
1985   Prehistoric Human Skeletal Remains Excavated in Shoofly Village during 1984 and 1985: A First Interim Report. Manuscript on file, Department of Anthropology, Arizona State University, Tempe.

James, Steven R.
1991   Protohistoric and Historical Background. In *The Archaeology of Star Valley, Arizona: Variation in Small Communities,* edited by Owen Lindauer, Ronna J. Bradley, and Charles L. Redman, pp. 35–41. Anthropological Field Studies No. 24, Department of Anthropology, Arizona State University, Tempe.

1992   Regional Variation in Pueblo Household Use of Space in the American Southwest. Ph.D. dissertation, Department of Anthropology, Arizona State University, Tempe.

Jeter, Marvin D.
1978   Archaeological Investigation of the Payson Parcel, Haverfield Land Exchange, Tonto National Forest, Arizona. Manuscript on file, Department of Anthropology, Arizona State University, Tempe.

Kelly, Roger E.
1969   An Archaeological Survey in the Payson Basin, Central Arizona. *Plateau* 42(1):46–55.

Lekson, Stephen H.
1991 Settlement Patterns and the Chaco Region. In *Chaco and Hohokam: Prehistoric Regional Systems in the American Southwest,* edited by Patricia L. Crown and W. James Judge, pp. 31-57. School of American Research Press, Santa Fe.

Li, Kuang-Ti
1988 Prehistoric Settlement Pattern in the Payson Area. Master's thesis, Department of Anthropology, Arizona State University, Tempe.

Lightfoot, Kent G., David R. Abbott, and Marcey Prager-Bergman
1977 The West Payson Survey. Manuscript on file, Department of Anthropology, Arizona State University, Tempe.

Lindauer, Owen
1991a Inferring Function from Plainware Ceramics. In *The Archaeology of Star Valley, Arizona: Variation in Small Communities,* edited by Owen Lindauer, Ronna J. Bradley, and Charles L. Redman, pp. 539-55. Anthropological Field Studies No. 24, Department of Anthropology, Arizona State University, Tempe.

1991b Issues in Establishing a Chronology for Star Valley. In *The Archaeology of Star Valley, Arizona: Variation in Small Communities,* edited by Owen Lindauer, Ronna J. Bradley, and Charles L. Redman, pp. 339-71. Anthropological Field Studies No. 24, Department of Anthropology, Arizona State University, Tempe.

1991c Prehistoric Culture History in Star Valley. In *The Archaeology of Star Valley, Arizona: Variation in Small Communities,* edited by Owen Lindauer, Ronna J. Bradley, and Charles L. Redman, pp. 31-35. Anthropological Field Studies No. 24, Department of Anthropology, Arizona State University, Tempe.

1991d Site AR-03-12-04-630 (TNF). In *The Archaeology of Star Valley, Arizona: Variation in Small Communities,* edited by Owen Lindauer, Ronna J. Bradley, and Charles L. Redman, pp. 234-40. Anthropological Field Studies No. 24, Department of Anthropology, Arizona State University, Tempe.

1991e Site AR-03-12-04-639 (TNF). In *The Archaeology of Star Valley, Arizona: Variation in Small Communities,* edited by Owen Lindauer, Ronna J. Bradley, and Charles L. Redman, pp. 240-56. Anthropological Field Studies No. 24, Department of Anthropology, Arizona State University, Tempe.

1991f Site AR-03-12-04-648 (TNF). In *The Archaeology of Star Valley, Arizona: Variation in Small Communities,* edited by Owen Lindauer, Ronna J. Bradley, and Charles L. Redman, pp. 114-126. Anthropological Field Studies No. 24, Department of Anthropology, Arizona State University, Tempe.

1992   Centralized Storage: Evidence from a Salado Platform Mound. In *Developing Perspectives on Tonto Basin Prehistory*, edited by Charles L. Redman, Glen E. Rice, and Kathryn Pedrick. Anthropological Field Studies No. 26, Department of Anthropology, Arizona State University, Tempe.

Lindauer, Owen, Ronna J. Bradley, and Charles L. Redman (editors)
1991   *The Archaeology of Star Valley, Arizona: Variation in Small Communities.* Anthropological Field Studies No. 24, Department of Anthropology, Arizona State University, Tempe.

Longacre, William A.
1970   *Archaeology as Anthropology: A Case Study.* Anthropological Papers of the University of Arizona 17. Tucson.

Lowe, Charles H.
1964   *Arizona's Natural Environment.* University of Arizona Press, Tucson.

Macnider, Barbara S., and Richard W. Effland, Jr.
1989   *Tonto National Forest Cultural Resources Assessment and Management Plan.* Cultural Resources Inventory Report 89–235, Archaeological Consulting Services, Phoenix.

McGregor, John C.
1977   *Southwestern Archaeology.* University of Illinois Press, Urbana.

McGuire, Thomas R.
1980   *Mixed-Bloods, Apaches, and Cattle Barons: Documents for a History of the Livestock Economy on the White Mountain Reservation, Arizona.* Arizona State Museum Archaeological Series No. 142, Tucson.

Miller, JoAnne
1990   Subsistence Practices at Shoofly Village AZ 0:11:6 (ASU): The Botanical Evidence. Master's thesis, Department of Anthropology, Arizona State University, Tempe.

1991   Flotation Analysis. In *The Archaeology of Star Valley, Arizona: Variation in Small Communities,* edited by Owen Lindauer, Ronna J. Bradley, and Charles L. Redman, pp. 379–93. Anthropological Field Studies No. 24, Department of Anthropology, Arizona State University, Tempe.

Minnis, Paul E., and Charles L. Redman (editors)
1990   *Perspectives on Southwestern Prehistory.* Westview Press, Boulder, Colorado.

Montero, Laurene G.
1988   Site AR-03-12-04-137 (TNF). In *Continuing Studies in Payson Prehistory*, edited by John W. Hohmann and Charles L. Redman, pp. 114–18. Anthropological Field Studies No. 21, Department of Anthropology, Arizona State University, Tempe.

1989   Architectural Complexity and the Use of Rooms at Shoofly Village. Master's thesis, Department of Anthropology, Arizona State University, Tempe.

Morris, Ann Axtell
1933   *Digging in the Southwest.* E. M. Hale and Co., Chicago.

Morris, Louisa Ann
1990   A Bioarchaeological Analysis of Five Adult Burials from Schoofly Village (AZ 0:11:16), Payson, Arizona. B.A. honor's thesis, Department of Anthropology, Arizona State University, Tempe.

Most, Rachel
1975   A Preliminary Report on Shoofly Village. In Preliminary Report on the 1975 Season Investigations, Payson Ranger District, Tonto National Forest, edited by A. E. Dittert, Jr. Manuscript on file, Department of Anthropology, Arizona State University, Tempe.

Nials, Fred L., David A. Gregory, and Donald A. Graybill
1989   Salt River Streamflow and Hohokam Irrigation Systems. In *The 1982–84 Excavations at Las Colinas: Environment and Subsistence,* edited by Donald A. Graybill, David A. Gregory, Fred L. Nials, Suzanne K. Fish, Charles H. Miksicek, Robert E. Gasser, and Christine R. Szuter. pp. 59–76. Arizona State Museum, Archaeological Series 162 (5), University of Arizona, Tucson.

Northern Gila County Historical Society (NGCHS)
1984   *The Rim Country History.* Rim Country Printery, Payson, Arizona.

Olson, Alan P., and Frances S. Olson
1954   A Survey of the Pine-Payson Area, Central Arizona. Manuscript on file, Arizona State Museum, University of Arizona, Tucson.

Peck, Fred
1956   An Archaeological Reconnaissance of the East Verde River in Central Arizona. Master's thesis, Department of Anthropology, University of Arizona, Tucson.

Plog, Stephen
1980   *Stylistic Variation in Prehistoric Ceramics: Design Analysis in the American Southwest.* Cambridge University Press, Cambridge.

Redman, Charles L.
1978   *The Rise of Civilization: From Early Farmers to Urban Society in the Ancient Near East.* W. H. Freeman and Co., San Francisco.
1987   Surface Collection, Sampling, and Research Design: A Retrospective. *American Antiquity* 52(2):249–65.
1989   Archaeology Returns to the Public. *Native Peoples* (Spring 1989): 28–33.
1992   The Impact of Food Production. *Humans and the Environment,* edited by J. Firor and J. Jacobsen, Westview Press, Boulder, Colorado.

Redman, Charles L., Ronna J. Bradley, and Owen Lindauer (editors)
1987   The 1987 Field Season at Shoofly Village. A Preliminary Report Submitted to the Tonto National Forest and the State Historic Preservation Officer of Arizona. Department of Anthropology, Arizona State University, Tempe.

Redman, Charles L., and John W. Hohmann (editors)
1986   *Small Site Variability in the Payson Region: the FLEX Land Exchange.* Anthropological Field Studies Number 11, Office of Cultural Resource Management, Department of Anthropology, Arizona State University, Tempe.

Redman, Charles L., Glen E. Rice, and Kathryn Pedrick (editors)
1992   *Developing Perspectives on Tonto Basin Prehistory.* Anthropological Field Studies No. 26, Department of Anthropology, Arizona State University, Tempe.

Renfrew, Colin
1975   Trade as Action at a Distance: Questions of Integration and Communication. In *Ancient Civilization and Trade,* edited by Jeremy A. Sabloff and C. C. Lamberg-Karlovsky, pp. 3–59. University of New Mexico Press, Albuquerque.

Rice, Glen E.
1984   Life in Hohokam Courtyards. *Arizona Highways Magazine* 60(2):1–2.

Rice, Glen E. (editor)
1990   *A Design for Salado Research. Roosevelt Platform Mound Study.* Roosevelt Monograph Series 1, Anthropological Field Studies No. 22, Department of Anthropology, Arizona State University, Tempe.

Rogge, A. E. (editor)
1989   *Fighting Indiana Jones in Arizona.* 1988 Proceedings of the American Society for Conservation Archaeology. Portales, New Mexico.

Sellers, William D. and Richard H. Hill (editors)
1974   *Arizona Climate 1931-1972.* University of Arizona Press, Tucson.

Sellers, William D., Richard H. Hill, and M. Sanderson-Rae
1985   *Arizona Climate: The First Hundred Years.* University of Arizona Press, Tucson.

Shackley, M. Steven
1986   X-Ray Fluorescence (XRF) Analysis of Obsidian Artifacts from Shoofly Ruin, Central Arizona. Manuscript on file, Department of Anthropology, Arizona State University, Tempe.

Simon, Arleyn W.
1988   Integrated Ceramic Analysis: An Investigation of Intersite Relationships in Central Arizona. Ph.D. dissertation, Department of Anthropology, Arizona State University, Tempe.

Simon, Arleyn W., and James Burton
1991   Star Valley Plainware Ceramic Analysis. In *The Archaeology of Star Valley, Arizona: Variation in Small Communities,* edited by Owen Lindauer, Ronna J. Bradley, and Charles L. Redman, pp. 469–539. Anthropological Field Studies No. 24, Department of Anthropology, Arizona State University, Tempe.

Snow, David H.
1991   Upland Prehistoric Maize Agriculture in the Eastern Rio Grande and its Peripheries. In *Farmers, Hunters, and Colonists,* edited by K. Spielmann, pp. 71–88. University of Arizona Press, Tucson.

Spoerl, Patricia, and George Gummerman (editors)
1983   *Prehistoric Cultural Development in Central Arizona: Archaeology of the Upper New River Region.* Occasional Paper No. 5, Center for Archaeological Investigations, Southern Illinois University, Carbondale.

Stafford, Barbara D.
1979   A Techno-Functional Study of Lithics from Payson, Arizona. Ph.D. dissertation, Department of Anthropology, Arizona State University, Tempe.

Stark, Barbara L.
1986   Origins of Food Production in the New World. In *American Archaeology Past and Future: A Celebration of the Society for American Archaeology 1935-1985,* edited by David J. Meltzer, Don D. Fowler, and Jeremy A. Sabloff, pp. 277–321. Smithsonian Institution Press, Washington, D.C.

Stone, Tammy T.
    1991   Groundstone. In *The Archaeology of Star Valley, Arizona: Variation in Small Communities*, edited by Owen Lindauer, Ronna J. Bradley, and Charles L. Redman, pp. 446–64. Anthropological Field Studies No. 24, Department of Anthropology, Arizona State University, Tempe.

Stone, Tammy T., and Ronna J. Bradley
    1991   A Characterization of Projectile Points from the Star Valley and Payson Region. In *The Archaeology of Star Valley, Arizona: Variation in Small Communities*, edited by Owen Lindauer, Ronna J. Bradley, and Charles L. Redman, pp. 437–46. Anthropological Field Studies No. 24, Department of Anthropology, Arizona State University, Tempe.

Stuiver, Minze, and B. Becker
    1986   High-Precision Calibration Decodal Calibration of the Radiocarbon Time Scale, A.D. 1950–2500 B.C. *Radiocarbon* 28:863–910.

Upham, Steadman
    1982   *Polities and Power: An Economic and Political History of the Western Pueblo*. Academic Press, New York.

Upham, Steadman, Kent G. Lightfoot, and Roberta A. Jewett (editors)
    1989   *The Sociopolitical Structure of Prehistoric Southwestern Societies*. Westview Press, Boulder, Colorado.

Wilcox, David R., and Charles Sternberg
    1983   *Hohokam Ballcourts and Their Interpretation*. Arizona State Museum Archaeological Series No. 160. University of Arizona, Tucson.

Willey, Gordon R. (editor)
    1974   *Archaeological Research in Retrospect*. Winthrop and Publishers, Cambridge, Massachusetts.

Wills, W. H.
    1988   *Early Prehistoric Agriculture in the American Southwest*. School of American Research Press, Santa Fe.

Wobst, H. M.
    1977   Stylistic Behavior and Information Exchange. In *Papers for the Director: Research Essays in Honor of James B. Griffen*, edited by C. Cleland, pp. 317–42. Anthropological Papers No. 61, University of Michigan, Museum of Anthropology, Ann Arbor.

Wood, J. Scott
    1985   Second Foundation: Settlement Patterns and Agriculture in the Northeastern Hohokam Periphery, Central Arizona. Manuscript on file, Tonto National Forest, Phoenix.

1987   Checklist of Pottery Types for the Tonto National Forest: An
        Introduction to the Archeological Ceramics of Central Arizona.
        The Arizona Archaeologist 21, Arizona Archaeological Society,
        Phoenix.

Woolley, L.
1954   *Excavations at Ur.* Benn, London.

Index

abandonment, 10, 15, 34, 42, 85, 115, 146, 147, 155, 157, 159, 167, 168
Abert's squirrel, 150, 151 (fig.)
absolute dating, 40
Adams, Robert McC., 14
agave, 33, 138, 144, 145, 178-179 (table)
agriculture, 18, 26, 33, 38, 142, 143, 156, 168; growing season, 24; hamlet, 17, 98, 145-146, 160, 171; household, 17, 105, 106, 145, 158, 171; irrigation, 11, 157, 168, 169; production zone, 47; rainfall-watered, 13, 16-17, 22, 24, 39 (table), 47, 156-157, 168; village, 17, 39 (table), 47, 145, 161, 171
alligator juniper (*Juniperus deppeana*), 26
alluvium, 28, 30. *See also* creek zone
alpine meadows, 21
American Indians: contemporary, 2, 3, 10, 11, 33-34, 113; prehistoric, 9, 10-11, 13
amphibians, 27, 180 (table)
Anasazi cultural tradition, 2, 11, 12 (fig.), 14, 15-16, 47, 64, 161, 164, 165, 166
Anderson Mesa, 168
antelope (*Antilocapra americana*), 27, 33
antelope jackrabbit, 150, 151 (fig.)
anvils, 78, 135, 137
Apaches, 33-35, 113
archaeological monuments, 10, 11
archaeological national parks, 10
archaeological research center, 51
archaeology, 5-6, 59, 54; and the public, 7-8. *See also* Southwest archaeology
archaeomagnetic measurement, 40, 176-177 (table)
Archaic phase, 39 (table), 41, 113
architectural styles, 3, 15, 18, 43, 45, 46, 47, 58, 155, 169

argillite, 76, 128 (fig.), 139, 140 (fig.)
Arizona, 10; climatic zones, 23-24; natural resources, 19; rainfall, 12, 21, 22-23; temperature, 23-24. *See also* Payson-Star Valley area; Shoofly Village Ruins; Southwest archaeology
Arizona Archaeological Society, 7, 39 (table), 50
Arizona State Museum excavations, 4
Arizona State University (ASU), 1, 53, 143, 172; field school excavations, 4-6, 39 (table), 59
arrow straightener, 92-93 (figs.), 135
arroyos, 21, 37, 53, 168
artifact scatters, 3, 5, 43, 106, 111
aster, 178-179 (table)
ASU. *See* Arizona State University
Athapaskan speakers, 33
Atwell, Karen C., 143
autonomy. *See* hamlets; households; villages; Shoofly Village Ruins, social groups
awls: bone, 136 (fig.), 138, 152
axes: argillite, 139; grooved, 65-66; polished, 78, 135-137

badgers, 27
ball courts, 164
basalt, 28, 29 (fig.), 64, 65, 70, 131, 134
base camps, 33, 39 (table), 41, 45
"basin and range" region, 20
basin sites, 43
baskets, 163
beads, 138, 139
beans, 144, 145, 178-179 (table)
bear, 27, 150
bedrock mortars, 57, 58 (photo), 79, 114, 117